...COPING WITH RAINY DAYS

SUBESH RAMJATTAN

SECOND EDITION

AGEING HAS A SILVER LINING

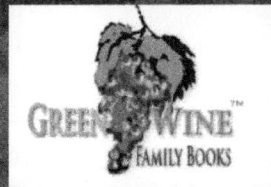

GREEN WINE™
FAMILY BOOKS

GlobalEdAdvance
Press

AGEING HAS A SILVER LINING: Coping with Rainy Days
Second Edition

Copyright © 2015, 2018 by Subesh Ramjattan

Library of Congress Control Number: 2014932061
Ramjattan, Subesh 1951—
Ageing Has a Silver Lining

ISBN 978-1-935434-65-8

Subject Codes and Description: 1: SEL 005000: Self-Help: Ageing
2: FAM 005000 Family & Relationships: Ageing-General; 3: SOC
013000: Gerontology.

NOTE: This book uses British English spelling *Ageing* with the
exception of certain Appendices using American English spelling
Aging.

Cover Design: Global Graphics – photograph by Gloria G. Green

Printed in Australia, Brazil, Canada, China, EU, Germany, India, Italy,
Poland, Russia, South Korea, UK, and USA

Available at all Espresso Book Machines and anywhere good books
are sold.

Published by
GreenWine Family Books

**A division of
GlobalEdAdvancePRESS**

www.gea-books.com

With deep affection,
This book is dedicated to

Mama

(Rosie Latchmin Ramjattan)

1927 — 2013

May her family, friends, and all
Who read this book remember her
Life, lessons, and legacy.*

(See Chapter Ten and Appendix Five)

PREFACE TO THE SECOND EDITION

*E*xcerpts from my recent address at UWI, "Take Back the Moral High Ground," were used to create a Preface for this Second Edition of *Ageing Has A Silver Lining*. Why? Because my heart and understanding remain the same as when I was first prompted to write this book. Most professionals have become accustomed to the "moral darkness" around us and normally do not see the needs of children, adults, or the elderly of the Nation. When it comes to morality and ethics, charity and generosity in support of the needy, we must take back the moral high ground clearly held by those who established this Nation.

Recently, I was reminded of the Hippocratic Oath. It is a system of moral principles that apply values and judgments to the practice of medicine, a most honorable profession. Other professions have similar documents. Those with expertise and resources must join the effort to make moral citizens of the children and solicit the assistance of the business community and non-profit entities to join with the government to meet the basic needs of all citizens. We must get professionals, parents, faith-based entities, leaders, and elected officials reading the same page and singing the same tune to demonstrate a spirit of cooperation.

We must utilize the expertise and energy of all professions in assisting the present and the next generation. It is immoral to avoid this responsibility; it is less than humane to fail in our responsibility to the generation that brought us into this world, invested in our growing years, gave us a moral compass, provided the encouragement for an adequate education, and gave us the will to grow into productive citizens. To withhold care or resources from children, the poor, and the elderly is a gross injustice and a moral blight on any society. We must take back the moral high ground!

My personal concern for the less fortunate came from frequent statements by my mother: she would often say things such as, "Never look down at some-one unless you are willing to help them get up." This instilled in me a passionate commitment to assist the less fortunate, especially neglected children, dysfunctional families, those with limited access to higher education, and the elderly in need of housing and care. I see this as a moral obligation. We all should remember that opportunity equals obligation.

Perhaps the historic professions of religion, law and medicine have the most opportunities to meet this moral obligation. One must never pass up an opportunity to assist others on their journey. We must all develop a sense of duty and responsibility to take back the moral high ground established by the early leaders of this Nation. We owe a debt for our own upbringing. Not just a general sense of indebtedness, but a grateful heart for family, the opportunity for education, good friends and a stable government. We must all become aware of the opportunities around us to make a difference. And remember, "You don't have to make news headlines to make a difference in the lives of others."

There is a story about an old man in a small town, called the "Lamplighter." Each night he would light the gas lamp at the street corner. The old gas lamps made only a small light on the dark street. As the Lamplighter made his rounds, it appeared he was knocking holes in the darkness. This is an example of what one person could do. And a good example for those who read this book: daily strive to knock holes in the darkness and enlighten the pathway to a better life for those in need with special concern for the elderly. At this moment in history, this is where we stand. Will you join men and women of good will and take the necessary steps to create a cooperative effort to take back the moral high ground and move this Nation forward into the light of reality. Dare we do less?

— **Subesh Ramjattan**

CONTENTS

PUBLISHER'S PREFACE

With a major change in lifestyle and focus as an adult, Subesh Ramjattan brought with him a varied history. His life narrative included growing up poor, with limited opportunities, educational struggles, early illness that included the loss of a kidney, the death of a younger brother, business problems, the use of alcohol, and marriage difficulties all contributed to his concern for the needy and disadvantaged. These growing up lessons, plus sacred writings about a loving and caring Man from Galilee produced a Subesh version of community service. This was enhanced by a frequent statement by his mother, **"Never look down at someone unless you are willing to help them get up."** This gradually instilled in Subesh a passionate commitment to assist the less fortunate, especially abandoned children and the needy elderly.

Ancient sacred writings recorded accounts of caring for children and narratives that demonstrated concern for the poor, the sick, and the dying. These revealed people who wept at the death of a friend, expressed love even for enemies, took the long view of life, and planned carefully for a legacy of followers to continue their good work. This appears to be the basis for service to the disadvantaged utilized in the work and community service of Subesh and his wife, Debra. According to the book, *The Anapausis Partnership* (2011), Debra Ramjattan shared a common back-ground experience and this informed her support for their work and service to the poor and needy.

The Ramjattan point of view encourages entrepreneurs to work in local communities. This unselfish attitude has produced, the Bridge of Hope childcare facility, a safe place for abused, abandoned, and disadvantaged children to grow, develop and bloom into productive citizens. The model of community service that produced the Bridge of Hope also developed the Anapausis Community Compound to serve the larger faith-based community in their search for a better life, improved relationships, and an enhanced quality of family life. The practical aspects of this model include a quality of life component shared with couples and individuals struggling with the normal adult difficulties and relationship issues in business and family life. The Anapausis Community also nurtured the OASIS UNIVERSITY, known as **O.A.S.I.S.** Institute of Higher Learning, or (**O.A.S.I.S.--O**mega **A**dvanced **S**chool for **I**nterdisciplinary **S**tudy) where Subesh served as Chairman of the Board for the first decade. The **O.A.S.I.S.** mission is to produce positive social change through graduate education for the Caribbean Region.

The present high point of the Ramjattan charitable effort is Olive's House, a four-stage project to serve the needs of the elderly and designed to serve as a model and inspiration for other senior facilities. This is indeed a genuine concern for the disadvantaged with the goal of improving the quality of life that spans the needs of childhood, the growing adult years, the final decades of graceful ageing, and compassionate end of life care. The objective is to insure a Silver Lining to the dark clouds that often surround the ageing process.

This book, *Ageing Has a Silver Lining*, is part of a noble effort on the part of Subesh and Debra Ramjattan to maintain a concern for disadvantaged children, support for business, families, higher education, and make provision for the needs of the elderly. Sandwiched between the children and the elderly is the work of The Anapausis Community that provides family housing, and operational space for multiple endeavors from children and youth activities, family life, marriage enrichment, faith-based functions, and the ongoing activities of higher education.

In the summer of 2014, growing out of concern for the needs of women, an initiative **Global Women's Inter-reliant NETWORK** (GlobalWIN) was launched to cultivate the Divine Nurturing Attribute of Women in Trinidad and Tobago and the Caribbean Region. In the fall of 2014, the Anapausis

Community initiated the ANAPAUSIS Together/Strong NETWORK, a strategy to organize men for moral excellence and transparency in belief and conduct and cultivate mutual support for others in business and non-profit services.

— Hollis L. Green, ThD, PhD, DLitt.

Publisher's Note: This book uses the British spelling of "ageing."

Ageing (British English) or **aging** (American English) is the accumulation of changes in a person over time.[1] Ageing in humans refers to a multidimensional process of physical, psychological, and social change. Some dimensions of ageing grow and expand over time, while others decline. Reaction time, for example, may slow with age, while knowledge of world events and wisdom may expand. Research shows that even late in life, potential exists for physical, mental, and social growth and development.[2]Ageing is an important part of all human societies reflecting the biological changes that occur, but also reflecting cultural and societal conventions. Roughly 100,000 people worldwide die each day of age-related causes.[3]

Age is measured chronologically and a person's birthday is often an important event. However the term "ageing" is somewhat ambiguous. Distinctions may be made between "universal ageing" (age changes that all people share) and "probabilistic ageing" (age changes that may happen to some, but not all people as they grow older including diseases such as type two diabetes). Chronological ageing may also be distinguished from "social ageing" (cultural age-expectations of how people should act as they grow older) and "biological ageing" (an organism's physical state as it ages).[4] There is also a distinction between "proximal ageing" (age-based effects that come about because of factors in the recent past) and "distal ageing" (age-based differences that can be traced back to a cause early in person's life, such as childhood poliomyelitis).

(For more data See http://en.wikipedia.org/wiki/Ageing)

Papalia, Diane. Olds, Sally W., Feldman, Ruth D. (2004) "Physical and Cognitive Development in Late Adulthood". Human Development. Mc-Graw Hill.

De Grey, Aubrey D.N.J (2007). "Life Span Extension Research and Public Debate: Societal Considerations". Studies in Ethics, Law, and Technology.

Phillips, Judith, Kristine Ajrouch, and Sarah Hillcoat-Nallétamby, (2010) Key Concepts in Social Gerontology. SAGE Publications.

Stuart-Hamilton, Ian (2006). The Psychology of Ageing: An Introduction. London: Jessica Kingsley Publishers.

ENDORSEMENT: Dr. Myles Munroe, Chairman
International Third World Leaders Association

*Aging Has a Silver Lining i*s an erudite, eloquent, and immensely thought-provoking work that gets to the heart of loving the human from birth to death. This demonstrates and addresses the subject with a profound simplicity that even the least among us can comprehend.

Aging Has a Silver Lining is indispensable reading for anyone who wants to understand how to serve the weakest and most vulnerable among us effectively. This is a profound authoritative work with a living example of loving the image of God and its principles spans the wisdom of the ages and yet breaks new ground in its approach to understanding the very important subject of serving the young and old among us. This book will possibly become a classic in this and the next generation.

This exceptional work **is one of the most profound, practical, principle-centered** approaches to this subject of serving and giving to humanity I have read in a long time. The author's approach to this timely issue brings a fresh breath of air that captivates the heart, engages the mind and inspires the spirit of the reader. Enjoy the journey through these pages and be transformed.

ENDORSEMENT: Professor Lee Elliott,
Director, The Wonderful Life Project

Ageing Has a Silver Lining certainly is relevant to one area of research I have pursued for several years to determine how elders (and I am one) can find meaning in their life. I was honored to review this book and provide some comments.

In *Ageing Has a Silver Lining*, Subesh Ramjattan has provided a book with an intriguing blend of science, philosophy, and homespun wisdom on ways that we might live the last years of our life so that we might find the meaning in life that we seek. He incorporates guidance ranging from diet and exercise to ways we might experience death with dignity. This book will be useful to a great many people.

A common question among the elderly is "Did my life have meaning and did I make a difference?" A dear friend, Jan Thayer, who worked in eldercare most of her life observed that only a few, at the time of their death, felt they made a difference. They often expressed that their living really did not matter. In effect, most of us end our lives believing we did not make a difference.

I also would like to comment on the decision to locate the eldercare facility, Olive House, close to the childcare facility, Bridge of Hope. This is brilliant. There is strong evidence that a key requirement for children to become resilient is that they feel loved. The elders of Olive House certainly will provide such care and love. In doing so, the elders will be more likely to have a sense of purpose and meaning during their final days. Locating the facilities and, therefore, the residents of each in such a manner is a great act of compassion and reflects deep understanding of the people to whom Subesh has dedicated his life. I wish him great success.

FOREWORD

*A*geing is a relevant and interesting topic. From a review of the contents, it is evident the author did a lot of research. Observing his parents ageing process, Subesh Ramjattan was able to identify some significant challenges of the progression. This book is a "must have" especially since ageing disturbs all of us. Some forecast if you live to age 62, you will probably make it to 92. The certain fact: the senior population is growing at a rapid rate. It is critical that we develop a fresh appreciation and an understanding of the implications of ageing.

The author has adequately dealt with the needs of the elderly, the journey, the moods, and the feeling of loneliness. A recent World Health Organization (WHO) forecast warned that by 2020 the major cause for disease and death will be complications from depression. As one grows older and friends, family and peers die, loneliness and depression overwhelms many. Can you identify a correlation with depression and ageing? How do you deal with the process? The data presented by Dr. Ramjattan comes from both research and experience. He uses information from different cultures and nations in putting together a "Silver Lining" for the ageing process.

Billy Graham, at age 93, in the opening paragraph of *Nearing Home*, wrote, "I never thought I would live to be this old," he continued, "growing old has been the greatest *surprise* of my life." More reason to read this book on ageing, and to use and pass on what you learn. Many live the Epicurean Life Style "…eat, drink and be merry for tomorrow we die." Obviously, we will be living longer, and the preparation for this journey as a child, parent, grandparent, must not take us by surprise. Can I live a life of dignity after I retire or do I have to depend on the required service of others? Should I include in my planning the preparation of resources to assist my ageing parents, myself, and also my dependants?

This book challenges all during lifespan development: the young, the middle aged and of course the seniors. I am extremely excited about this well thought out compilation of practical ideas about ageing. I have seen the concepts of this book unfold before my eyes as a life-planner and as a son. My dad died at age 99 and my mother at age 86. In my profession of Life Planning, it is clear that the difficult age is truly when you are "too tired to work, and too poor to quit."

Prepare yourself for an exciting experience. Buckle up as you get on the ageing roller coaster. It matters not where you sit, or from which viewpoint you see the process. This book will enrich and empower you to rethink and plan for this predictable stage of life.

— Trevor Rex Baddaloo
Certified Human Behaviour Consultant,
Regional Manager – South – The Maritime Financial Group
"The Home for Champions"

Author's Introduction

My personal concern for the less fortunate came from frequent statements by my mother. This gradually produced a personal commitment to assist the less fortunate, especially abandoned children, dysfunctional families, and the needs of the elderly. I see this as a moral obligation. We must all remember that opportunity equals obligation. We must never pass up a chance to assist others on their journey. We must all develop a sense of duty and responsibility to take back the moral high ground so nobly established by our forefathers. We owe a debt for our own upbringing. Not just a sense of indebtedness, but a grateful heart for family, friends and a stable government. We must all become aware of the opportunities around us to make a difference. And remember, **"You don't have to make headlines to make a difference in the lives of others."**

My passion is to improve the quality of life for the elderly. Most people do not adequately invest the time or resources to ensure that plans are in place for the final decades of life. This book is designed to encourage everyone to seek the right counsel and guidance from trusted friends and professionals in the field of ageing to maintain a quality of life during their final years. The silver lining to the clouds of ageing will not automatically appear; there must be a plan in place. When adequate plans are in place, there will be a peace of mind as the elderly face the final decades of life. Quantity of years is not the issue; the quality of those years is what counts. Plans can reduce the possibility that one will live longer, but enjoy life less.

We must not become accustomed to the "moral darkness" and neglect the seniors among us. When it comes to charity and generosity in support of the elderly, we must take back the moral high ground previously established. In the past, adult children felt an obligation and a passion to care for their parents. Sadly, this is not the case in many families. Consequently, others must make provision to care for the elderly among us. The deteriorating family environment and the neglect of the elderly has become a moral blight on society.

Those with expertise and resources must join the effort to care for the elderly and solicit the assistance of the business and faith-based communities to join the government in meeting the needs of the ageing population. We must utilize the expertise and energy of the community in assisting the next generation. It is immoral to avoid this responsibility; it is less than humane to fail in care for the generation that brought us into this world, invested in our growing years, gave us a moral compass, provided encouragement for an adequate education, and gave us a boost to start a productive adult life. To withhold care or resources from seniors is a gross injustice and a sign of moral decline in society. We must take back the moral high ground!

My intention is to see that the wisdom and talents of the elderly are captured and put to good use. The expertise of seniors must not be lost to the grave. Most people live longer than previous generations and some say "Sixty is the new forty." How we plan will determine the quality of life during those bonus years. What we do and how we live those extra decades may well determine whether there are silver linings to the ageing clouds or despair and disappointment. Hopefully, this book will assist you and your family to better understand the process of ageing and adequately plan for those extra years.

How can we use our resources to be a blessing to others? How can we surround ourselves with people who can build us up and use our knowledge and expertise to avoid the dark clouds of ageing? The elderly must remain active and useful. When one gets tired doing nothing there is no place to stop and rest. Could this be why tired old folks die? Retiring and doing nothing will bring a speedy deterioration to the quality of life and premature death will result. Physics teaches us that "a body in motion remains in motion and that a body at rest remains at rest." Encouragement and fellowship from family and friends are essential to avoid being depressed and lonely. A simple pledge written many years ago by a previous generation provides my countrymen with guidelines for a quality of life:

> *I solemnly pledge to dedicate my life*
> *To the service of my God and my country*
> *I will honour my parents, my teachers,*
> *My leaders and my elders,*
> *And those in authority.*
>
> *I will be clean and honest*
> *In all my thoughts, my words and my deeds*
> *I will strive in everything I do,*
> *To work together with my fellow man*
> *Of every creed and race,*
> *For the greater happiness of all*
> *And the honour and glory of my country.*

Perhaps lawmakers should revise retirement regulations and permit the elderly to better share their knowledge and experience with the younger generation so that the past struggles will enhance the young and the lessons of the past will multiply and not vanish as vapor. A simple plan for greatness is expressed in these words of Mahatma Gandhi ***"Man becomes great exactly in the degree in which he works for the welfare of his fellowman."***

— Subesh Ramjattan, DHL, DLitt

Wisdom OF THE AGES
MUST BE PASSED ON
TO THE NEXT GENERATION.

1

PLANNING
FOR THE AGEING PROCESS

Flexible Planning

One ageing gentleman working hard at planning the last decades of his life, fell asleep. He dreamed that he found a message washed to shore in a bottle that read "Write your plans in pencil and give *Me* the eraser. There may be something better, nicer, and more to your liking in your future." The note was signed God. Most elderly will not have such an experience, but it is always good to be flexible in planning your future. It is helpful to bring family, trusted friends, professional planners, and Providence into the planning process.

A First Time Journey

The ageing process is a first time journey and each person must make the best of it. The fear of the unknown is ever present as one makes this one-way march toward the setting sun. It is a journey never made before and will not be repeated. It is an anxious time; there are no second go a rounds, retakes or "I'll do better the next time." It is best to make good plans for this long trip toward the sunset. If individuals do not plan their future, someone else will. The plans of others may not adequately prepare the elderly for this special journey. Could this be a partial explanation for the unhappiness among the ageing population? Parents and grandparents deserve a better chance. What can we do to add grace to the ageing process?

Ageing Gracefully

Life-experience readily provides the resources, ability, and the opportunity for each person to age more gracefully than they otherwise would. There is a story of a gracious elderly lady who was mailing an old family sacred book to her younger brother for safe keeping. The postal clerk asked, "Is there anything breakable in here?" The firm and clear answer was "Only the words of the Prophets and a few Commandments." We must never break the chain of wisdom that reaches back to our heritage and the pages of sacred writings. Was this not the stabilizing force for our parents and grandparents?   In fact, it was the moral fiber that kept the world together during wars, famines, and natural disasters. We must not permit ageing to wipeout the good memories of the past or become a time of crisis for those we love and respect. Our personal future and the future of family is in our hands. There must be responsible planning.

The Final Assessment

Exams are painful for most students, especially a "final exam" that determines the grade for a course of study. Normally, there are no second chances for a final exam and many teachers, being true to their profession, give the grade the student actually earned.   In this matter, teachers often appear to be non-caring about the student's predicament. As students mature they realize that advance study and preparation can relieve this unpleasant and troublesome situation. Life itself becomes a learning and proving ground for the later years and for the final evaluation by a Higher Authority.   I remember a story of an ageing grandmother who was in an old rocking chair reading a big black sacred book when asked by a grandchild, "Granny what are you doing?" Her response, "I am cramming for my final exam." It would benefit everyone to make preparation for the later years and the ultimate end of life care and the final evaluation. Check with your insurance professional and see if policies and procedures are available to assist your final decades of life.

Dimensions of Ageing

The ageing process is a slow and often painful journey. Some dimensions of ageing grow and expand over time, while others decline. Reaction time may slow with age, while knowledge of world events and wisdom may expand. Research shows that even late in life, the potential exists for physical, mental, and social growth and development. Ageing is an important part of all human societies reflecting the biological changes (See **Appendix One**) that occur, but also revealing cultural and societal standards. Age is normally measured in full years; this means 365 days repeated annually giving the elderly many years to live a full and productive life. If medical science were to develop a Methuselah pill, even governments of the world would resist its use because if everyone lived to 100, it would destroy the safety nets prepared to care for the elderly and the poor. If individuals do not plan for their future and depend only on existing government allowances and company pensions to provide for health and safety, most will be disappointed with the quality of life during their final years. Serious consideration of options may demonstrate differences between a hopeful future and the alternatives resulting from delayed planning. The end of life planning is serious and requires the advice and counsel of professionals.

Positive and Respectful

The interaction between the elderly and the next generation ought to be both positive and respectful. There must be an orderliness of operation and practical arrangements for the benefit of all concerned. The efficiency and effectiveness of all services and programs must be strengthened and the benefits utilized to assist the whole family. When adults neglect the needs of children or elderly parents, family values are weakened or abandoned and the family suffers. To neglect children or the elderly is a moral disgrace; it is shameful and must never be permitted in a civilized society. The elderly have abilities and talents and have time to make a worthy contribution to both the family and society. This must be permitted and respected.

Contentment can be Great Gain

Contentment can be the soft inner voice at sundown saying, "Tomorrow is a new day, I will do better." In Sacred Scripture, St. Paul wrote "contentment is great gain (1 Timothy 6:6 EDNT). It seems being human causes one to worry about something, but ageing does not have to be a source of anxiety. For each moment of pain, there is a day of happiness. For each instant of worry, there is an hour of serenity. For each sleepless hour, there is night of rest. For each disappointment in life there is a compensating blessing. Life is not easy and it takes a toughness to live in a troubled world and participate in the marketplace of ideas and make a difference. Sir Winston Churchill wrote, "We have not journeyed all this way because we are made of sugar candy." Gandhi, in a commentary about capacity and will wrote, "Strength does not come from physical capacity. It comes from an indomitable will." One does not have to win a Nobel Prize to make a difference. A brief review of individuals who confronted the ageing process and made a worthy contribution could bring encouragement to those who fear the limitations of the ageing process.

Achievements at an Advanced Age

A few well-known individuals made major accomplishments in their later years. One of the most famous British personalities of the 20th Century was twice the Prime Minister of England, and served most effectively during the World War II era. Many people outside England tend to forget that Winston Churchill had a second session as Prime Minister at age 77. It was calculated that John Wesley delivered over 40,000 sermons and traveled 225,000 miles by horseback during the latter part of his life, from age 36 to 88. Elizabeth Wilson became interested in China at age 10, but did not arrive until thirty years later. Her situation was dangerous and harsh, but maturity and age proved to be an asset. She had arrived to do charity work in the Orient, where age was honored. Perhaps if others understood the accomplishments of the elderly, they too would see the Silver Lining of the ageing process. The list below provides other examples of achievements by seniors both male and female.

1. At 100, Grandma Moses was painting.
2. At 94, Bertrand Russell was active in international peace initiatives.
3. At 93, George Bernard Shaw wrote the play *Farfetched Fables.*
4. At 91, Eamon de Valera served as President of Ireland.
5. At 91, Adolph Zukon was chairman of Paramount Pictures.
6. At 90, Pablo Picasso was producing drawings and engravings.
7. At 89, Mary Baker Eddy was directing the Christian Science Church.
8. At 89, Arthur Rubinstein gave his greatest recitals in Carnegie Hall.
9. At 89, Albert Schweitzer headed a hospital in Africa.
10. At 88, Pablo Casals was giving cello concerts.
11. At 88, Michelangelo was still doing church architectural plans.
12. At 88, Konrad Adenauer was Chancellor of Germany.
13. At 85, Coco Chanel was the head of a fashion design firm.
14. At 84, Somerset Maugham wrote *Points of View.*
15. At 83, Aleksandr Kerensky wrote *Russia* and *History's Turning Point.*
16. At 82, Winston Churchill wrote a History of English Speaking People.
17. At 82, Leo Tolstoy wrote *I Cannot Be Silent.*
18. At 81, Benjamin Franklin worked to approve the U.S. Constitution.
19. At 81, Johann Wolfgang von Goethe finished *Faust.*
20. At 81, my friend, Hollis L. Green, finished the Evergreen Devotional New Testament, a 42-year project translating Koine' Greek into devotional English.
21. At 80, George Burns won an Academy Award for *The Sunshine Boys*
22. Perhaps you could add your own achievements to this list.

Seeds of Knowledge

Achievement does not rest or wait for a more convenient time; accomplishment depends on action not delay. Taking advantage of each opportunity to move forward toward stated goals is the reason for accomplishments in any culture. All of life is a learning process and many things are learned that enable seniors to be productive in their later years. Old age is not a time to go fishing and/or lethargically wait for the Grim Reaper; it should be a period of active participation in life. Seniors ought to continue doing the things that make a difference. With an opportunity and the proper atmosphere, the seniors could use all the knowledge and experience gained to make the last years productive and meaningful.

Don't Eat the Seed Corn

There is a story of a rural tribe that disappeared and academics discovered that during a drought the tribe ate their seed corn and had nothing to plant for a future crop. The wisdom of the ages must be passed on to the next generation. When family and friends neglect mealtime with seniors, it is similar to eating the seed corn and losing the past wisdom and knowledge that is needed to grow a new crop of prosperous individuals. Walking with family and friends as they age is an opportunity to gain wisdom added over a lifetime. When the young contemplate the passing of an ageing friend or family members, they should take a walk with them physically or emotionally and gain from their wisdom. Such a walk can become a Silver Lining for future cloudy days when their stored wisdom will be needed.

Resource for Services

A good example would be an organization of retired executives that provides volunteer services to new business and small operations unable to afford lawyers and consultants. Something with this essential character could be initiated in several communities to open doors of opportunity for service among the experienced elderly. Also, there are seniors with manual skills; such as, carpenters, masons, electricians, plumbers, and others that remain able bodied and willing to work and could become a resource for the community. This book suggests a new group of knowledgeable individuals dedicated to coaching and teaching the young their trade called **Exchange Trade Coaching (E.T.C).** The abbreviation **ETC** is a Latin expression meaning "*and other things.*" There are always "other things" seniors can teach the next generation.

Able-bodied Elderly

The able-bodied elderly need to know there are "*other things*" they can do rather than just get old. **E.T.C**. would be an organization that gathers and distributes information of value and guidance to individuals and eldercare facilities using volunteers with time-tested knowledge who donate coaching, mentoring, and tutoring relative to various aspects of business, community, family, and relationships. Hopefully, such a group would become a consultant operation and "pay it forward" by assisting others involved in community service and eldercare. The more the seniors use their life skills in a meaningful way, the less they notice their aches and pains.

Life Skills

Utilizing the **L. I. F. E. S. K. I. L. L. S.** of seniors could mean:

Legitimate grassroots

Involvement in projects

For the benefit of

Everyone, because

Society needs the

Knowledge

Imbedded in the

Lives and

Labor of able-bodied

Senior citizens….

Personal Initiative

Individual initiative can open the door to opportunities for continued productive work. In the past, many have made significant accomplishments after the world judged them unable or unworthy to continue participation. With the assistance of family, friends, wise businessmen, a compassionate society and a benevolent government, senior citizens could still use their life skills and make a positive contribution to society! Life skills are knowledge and actions used in the management of personal affairs. Society must not discard or neglect the use of the wisdom and proficiency of seniors. Utilized appropriately and responsibly, the life skills of mature citizens could bridge the gap between limited resources and human needs. Rather than becoming a burden to society, many seniors could be an economical labor force in a productive society.

Heart Changes

According to the Merck Manual of Geriatrics, several changes typically occur in the structure of the heart with age. These changes include increased thickness in the wall of the left ventricle in the lower heart; minor enlargement of the left ventricle itself; enlargement of the left atrium in the upper heart; and overall enlargement of the outline of the heart when viewed on an X-ray. Almost half of all people over age 70 experience an increase in the number of harmful, insoluble, fibrous proteins inside the heart. This can cause unavoidable changes in the heart. Ageing is a process and clearly causes unavoidable changes in the body, personal behavior, and lifestyle. Seniors have no time to waste!

Changes Vary

The cardiovascular system is a term used to describe the heart and its associated blood vessels--or circulatory system--which together pump oxygen-rich blood throughout the body and retrieve oxygen-depleted blood for replenishment in the lungs. During the ageing process, normal changes in the cardiovascular system tend to reduce blood flow in the body. However, the extent of these changes can vary considerably, and may be diminished with regular exercise. Regular exercise becomes a Silver Lining to the changes during the ageing process and extends the usefulness of seniors.

Increased Risks

In combination, the changes in the cardiovascular system associated with normal ageing can significantly increase the chances of experiencing high blood pressure, congestive heart failure, heart attack or stroke. A Utah State report discovered that reduced blood flow can also increase the chances of experiencing a toxic reaction to medications, as well as a diminished response to stress and a slower rate of healing from wounds or injuries. Seniors and their caregivers must be aware of these risks. Now you know. What will you do about exercise and extend your productive days?

Exercise a Consideration

The Merck Manual of Geriatrics notes that the medical personnel are not sure whether the cardiovascular diseases associated with ageing occur because of ageing itself, or are caused by other factors. In fact, it may be possible that elderly people experience these diseases more frequently because they have a longer overall timeframe of risk exposure than younger people. Additionally, not all ageing people undergo the same cardio-vascular changes. Regular exercise may potentially increase the oxygen exchange rate and reverse some decreases in cardiac function and diminish the effects of age-related blood vessel stiffness. Exercise and physical activity may bring a Silver Lining to the cloudy days of heart aches and pains. Give exercise some thought; it could make a difference! It is also good to remember the following words of Gandhi:

There is a sufficiency in the world for man's need
But not for man's greed.
There is nothing that wastes the body like worry,
And one who has any Faith in God
Should be ashamed to worry about anything
Whatsoever.

BEFORE YOU TALK,

listen.

BEFORE YOU REACT,

think.

BEFORE YOU CRITICIZE,

wait.

BEFORE YOU PRAY,

forgive.

BEFORE YOU QUIT,

try.

William Arthur Ward

2

DEALING
WITH THE ACHES AND PAINS

Life Improves with Age

A friend recently told his physician, "I am living longer, but enjoying it less." To which the doctor replied, "Sure there are adjustments to lifestyle, but aches and pains do not have to rob you of pleasures." With the use of common sense, life and living can improve with age. Regardless of aches and pains, one must learn to stop using their wings and reflect on their roots. The lessons learned in the past may be the answer to present difficulties.

Notwithstanding the aches and pains of ageing, the past both informs the present and the future. Knowing the struggle of ancestors and understanding their accomplishments as soldiers, doctors, lawyers, politicians, men of faith, women of worth, uncles of accomplishments, the courage of cousins, and sibling's achievements makes one proud of their personal and religious heritage. We have all learned that our children will outlive us and this will provide them with more time to reach their personal goals. Consequently, it is futile to overly concern ourselves about our children's future; it is more appropriate to remain concerned about our present existence. A primary lesson learned early was that life was less "what you do" and more "who you are." Maturing teaches us to never say "no" but to always say "Yes, but let me check my calendar." A positive outlook can mean good planning for the remaining decades of life.

Speak Straight Truth

Growing older teaches one to speak the straight truth in love regardless of where the chips fall.   Age brings more competence and confidence in many areas of life.   Learning that facts, data, and information are not yet knowledge, but must be used to answer a question or solve a problem before they become knowledge and mature into wisdom. A most significant aspect of ageing is learning that maturity and life-experience provide the understanding and good judgment to take care of personal business and to stay out of the business of others. Seniors may assist others with projects and programs without becoming the person in charge.   In fact, the best position is an advisor who is an arms-length away from the center of things.   A senior mechanic, an old navigator, or an experienced co-pilot can get the old plane flying, carrying cargo, and landing safely at a distant destination. Never underestimate talent and capability of a mature adult regardless of age.

Accumulation of Changes

Ageing appears to be the accumulation of changes in a person over time.   In humans there are physical, psychological, and social changes which occur to varying degrees and at different rates in individuals. As one ages, their reaction time may slow, but their wisdom and knowledge expands.   As physical strength lessens, expertise and understanding may increase. The Silver Lining to the ageing clouds becomes clear in the data, even late in life there is potential for physical, mental, and social growth and development. Notwithstanding this metaphor for achievement, many individuals worldwide still die each day of age-related issues. Some causes of death may be traced to an early childhood illness or accident and are not relevant to the majority of seniors. Although human life is valued in most societies, there is no willingness to fund research to extend life or a strong awareness of a need to delay the human ageing process. Therefore, the quality and quantity of life remains in the hands of each individual. Life must be something more than long. Quality of life has greater value than quantity for the ageing population who endure the aches and pains of growing older.

Chronological vs. Functional Age

Just as health issues are different with each individual, ageing is not the same for everyone. Some divide the ageing population into three categories: the young old (65–74), the middle old (75–84) and the oldest old (85+). It is clear that chronological age does not correlate perfectly with functional age, i.e. two people may be of the same age, but may differ in their mental and physical capacities. The way a nation, a government or an agency may classify age, may not coincide with individuals who have their own feeling about age. In fact, many believe age is a "state of mind." If this is true, then each individual mind-set will control much of the positive or negative feelings about the ageing process. The effort must be to remain as physically and mentally active and useful as possible regardless of age.

Change and Ageing

It is good for everyone to recognize that various changes take place in the human body as it ages: hearing and vision decline, muscle strength lessens, soft tissues such as skin and blood vessels become less flexible, and there is an overall decline in body tone. The effects of ageing can also influence the social and behavioral aspects of life. For example, the heart becomes less efficient with age making physical exercise and normal activities more difficult. This means that as one ages they must alter their physical fitness program to age-appropriate activities.

Most human organs perform less efficiently with advancing age. The average amount of blood pumped by the heart drops from about 6.9 liters per minute at age 20 to only 3.5 liters pumped per minute at age 85. For this same age range, the average amount of blood flowing through the kidneys drops by about one-half. Not all people experience decreased organ function at the same rate—some individuals have healthier hearts and kidneys at age 85 than others do at age 50. Multiple factors determine physical health: inherited genes, environment, lifestyle, diet and exercise over the previous twenty years. When these facts are understood, the elderly can face the ageing process with more confidence and with a healthy self-image. Also, others will be more able to see value in the continued involvement of seniors in community and family life.

The Immune System Changes

The immune system also changes with age. It is as important for all the elderly to be vaccinated against the flu and pneumonia as it is for young people to be vaccinated against childhood diseases. A healthy immune system protects the body against bacteria, viruses, and other harmful agents by producing disease-fighting proteins known as antibodies. A healthy immune system also prevents the growth of abnormal cells, which can become cancerous. With advancing age, the ability of the immune system to carry out these protective functions is diminished—the rate of antibody production may drop by as much as 80 percent as one reaches age 85. This less-effective immune system explains why a bout of influenza, which may make a young adult sick for a few days, can be fatal for an elderly person.

Most of the glands of the endocrine system, the organs that secrete hormones regulating such functions as metabolism, temperature, and blood sugar levels, retain their ability to function into advanced age. However, these glands often become less sensitive to the triggers that direct hormone secretion. In an ageing pancreas, for example, higher blood sugar levels are required to stimulate the release of insulin, a hormone that assists muscles in converting blood sugar to energy. Those aware of these changes can more readily protect their health. Knowledge of these facts can assist the caregivers of the elderly to better perform their duties.

Soap and Water

With current news about the threat of growth in antibiotic-resistant infections, even a friendly handshake can pass germs. Seniors do not have to look for a powerful weapon to protect their health from superbugs lurking everywhere; simple soap and water offers a good defense. In fact, because of research and discoveries, some of the companies which produce personal care products are phasing out some antibacterial products. This does not mean you can become careless, but it suggests that frequent hand washing could prevent some infections. However, soap and water will not cure aches and pains, but may prevent some infections and trips to the doctor.

Life Expectancy Increases

As the 21st century progresses, an ageing population is changing the face of the world. At the time the New World was revolting against England and Europe, colonists could expect to live to age 35, and only a few attaining the age of 65 or older. A hundred years later the life expectancy was 47; now the average life expectancy at birth is about 75, and a majority of all deaths occurring after age 65. When the baby-boomers, children of the "greatest generation," reach age 65, they will make up about twenty percent of the population. Barring a calamitous epidemic, catastrophic weather, or prolonged war, the percentage of persons over 65 will continue to grow in the generations ahead. This requires more advanced planning by individuals, families, and entities concerned about the housing and care of the elderly. The Silver Lining of the growth of the older population means that their expertise and wisdom will be available to assist the next generation. Increased life expectancy means individuals must personally plan for their extended life. Such important and personal matters must not be left to others.

Population Trends

Population growth is not confined to the Western Hemisphere. At the beginning of the 20th century, only one percent of the world's population lived past age 65. It is expected by 2050 about twenty percent of people in the developed nations of Western Europe, the Caribbean, and Japan, and more than fifteen percent of the population in developing nations will be 65 and older. This gives reason and urgency to the advanced planning for eldercare and programs to assist the ageing population.

Predictions

People speculating about global population predict that one-third of people over 65 will live in India or China. Other nations with huge populations of older people will include Russia, Indonesia, and Brazil. Life expectancy has increased due to improvements in medical care and advances in nutrition. Eventually the world's scientists may find a way to slow the ageing process itself. As the number of elderly increases, many challenges will be placed on governments and charity groups. As this trend continues, there will be opportunities to make fresh policy decisions about ageing based on realistic projections of the changing population.

Economic Issues

How will a large retired population living on social benefits and needing medical care impact the economic fortunes of the world? Will older people take resources away from younger generations? Will health care be rationed in favor of the young? Will the differing needs of older and younger people lead to inter-generational conflict? These are among the questions raised by the phenomenon some experts call the "new longevity."

Natural Effects of Ageing

The science that deals with ageing and the problems of the elderly covers the social and behavioral effects of the process. Those who scientifically view ageing study four distinct processes: chronological ageing, biological ageing, psychological ageing, and social ageing. The biological effects of ageing, such as the loss of flexibility in some tissues and the decline of organ function, can influence these social and behavioral effects. For example, the heart becomes less efficient as a person ages, making exercise more difficult. The cell* shows some of the natural effects of ageing. (*See Appendix Two for more data.)

Itching and Pain

Itching is low grade pain. With age the skin produces less natural oil that retains moisture. The itching or tingling of the skin that creates a desire to scratch may be only dry skin or a symptom of something else. Scratching may cause damage to the skin or create an infection.   Itching may occur anywhere on the body and the most common cause, other than dry skin or allergies, is psychological, and can normally be traced to anxiety, stress, or emotional issues. Scratching may be almost automatic, but one should avoid scratching and seek a remedy. A little soap and warm water may help, if this doesn't work, try some topical ointment or seek a medical evaluation. Otherwise the itching can become real pain.

Health Issues

One elderly lady explaining her situation shared "I don't have All-timers, I have Some-timers. Sometimes I just forget stuff." In addition to the aches and pains of ageing, the elderly face a growing list of health issues. Below are some of those frequently reported among the elderly. Managed health care is a goal of all facilities for the elderly.

- Alzheimer's & Dementia
- Ambulatory Difficulties
- Anger
- Cancer
- Depression
- Diabetes
- Diverticulitis
- Hearing Loss
- Heart Disease
- Incontinence
- Intellectual Function
- Lung Disease
- Memory Loss
- Nutritional Deficiency
- Osteoporosis
- Parkinson's Disease
- Vision and Hearing Disorders

In the present condition of the world, individuals must assume personal or family control of their health and manage their lifestyle in a manner that influences longevity.   Key factors under the control of the individual are diet, exercise, weight, and stress management.

Diet: Seniors should be encouraged to eat a little of everything, but not a lot of anything. Even if the taste is unfamiliar, new foods should be tried; in fact, after a few small portions of a new and different dish, the taste buds adjust to the flavor. It has been suggested that a diet that includes high levels of fruits, nuts, vegetables, and coffee may reduce mortality in older adults. It appears that the antioxidants from these foods increase longevity by neutralizing free radicals and decreasing the cell damage related to ageing. Tuna, salmon, sardines, and herring are sources of omega-3 fatty acids, which have properties that reduce most inflammation. It appears that less red meat and more whole grains, produce, fish, and nuts decreases the risk of developing diabetes. As one ages they never outgrow their need for calcium and vitamin D found in dairy products. No fat or low fat dairy foods can prevent osteoporosis and low bone mass that come with age. Refined sugar and processed or manufactured foods containing chemicals that work against longevity should be limited or eliminated.

Nature's Color-coded fruits and Vegetables

A proper diet is not easy, but nature has color-coded fruits and vegetables to simplify the process. A colorful diet is an easy way to get lots of vitamins and minerals. Fruits and vegetables get their colors from various antioxidants found in them. You may not be interested in the technical names for nutrition elements, but you need them just the same. Foods that promote healthy bones and teeth are leafy **greens** like romaine lettuce, cabbage, and Brussel sprouts. They are high in vitamin C and E, and a good source of iron. **Red** fruits and vegetables promote good health and brain function, and are high in vitamins A and C, with some manganese.

The colors that give fruits and vegetables visual appeal come from types of pigment: **carotenoids**, for **orange** and **yellow** vegetables; **flavonoids,** for **blue**, **red** and **cream** colors; and **chlorophyll**, makes things **green**. These colors also provide health and nutrition benefits. **Red** and **orange** fruits and vegetables are among the highest in vitamin C. Things **green** are a source for iron. **Blue** and **purple** foods have powerful antioxidants that may protect against cancer and heart disease. The dark pigmentation that causes some vegetables to appear **black** provides high levels of antioxidants.   However, **white** beans contain more iron, potassium and protein than black beans. Select a rainbow of colors for your plate and eat heartily and be healthy.

Weight: One small boy shared with his sister about the bathroom scale, "Don't step on that; it makes grown-ups cry." The pace of ageing increases as the number on the scale rises to the obesity range. Being overweight normally promotes Type 2 diabetes, increases the risk of heart disease and cancer. Weight also contributes to inflammation and degenerative arthritis and lung problems. This suggests that as one ages they should eat less and exercise more in an effort to shed excess pounds. This can be done by following a diet that has 25 percent fewer calories together with thirty minutes of moderate exercise. Proper diet and exercise lowers fasting insulin levels and body temperatures, both of which are indicators of longevity. Whether or not this practice will be a life-extender or not, those who practice proper diet and exercise will enjoy life more on a daily basis.

The English count their money in pounds, but their weight in "stones." One stone equals 14 pounds. Perhaps the English are right this time, extra weight is similar to carrying around "extra stones."   That makes 50 pounds overweight similar to carrying around a 50 pound rock. Beware of the hidden "stones" on the dinner table.   Since from little acorns mighty trees grow, perhaps from weighty "pebbles" in the diet comes a larger "stone" count in body weight.

Exercise: Regular moderate aerobic exercise can produce anti-ageing benefits. Aerobic activity gets you breathing harder and your heart beating faster. From 30 to 60 minutes four or five days a week can improve heart health, increase blood flow, tone muscles, reduce inflammation and lower the risk of cancer. If one is unable to do aerobics, a short walk after each meal, even a stroll of about 15 minutes soon after eating will keep blood sugar levels low and steady for the next three hours. The movement of the body causes the muscles to use more sugar from the bloodstream. There is a special program available on the Internet for those whose health or age will not permit aerobics; it is FREE to seniors who do not have insurance: *COTHenterprises.com*. (See Appendix Seven)

Regular exercise will assist the prevention of diabetes, age-related weight gain, and slow the process of dementia. According to Pam Peeke, M.D., regular physical activity assists metabolic function, preserves bone density, and overall health at the cellular level. Exercise normally produces anti-ageing benefits. An additional benefit: exercise can improve brain health and cognitive performance including memory, reasoning, intuition, and perception.

Stress: Chronic stress accelerates the ageing process. When one is constantly under pressure from daily activity or routine interaction, the body pumps out stress hormones that produce wear and tear on both mind and body and can overtime take a substantial toll on health. The difference between low and high stress can account for as much as a decade of ageing. Exercise and meditation are recognized as stress reducers that slow the ageing process. Bruce McEwen, the author of *The End of Stress as We Know It*, suggested that the best way to manage stress was to change personal habits and adopt a healthy lifestyle. This is best done by improving the amount and quality of sleep, having a healthy diet, and doing regular physical activity. An improved social life, together with a positive outlook on life, provides a better understanding and purpose for life. Utilizing the life skills of the seniors could make a difference in their struggle for self-confidence.

3

Struggling
with Self-confidence

Cradle to the Grave

Life matters at all ages and stages of life, from the cradle to the grave. Parents normally care for newborns as well as their other offspring regardless of the sacrifice. Equally, adult children have a responsibility to care for their parents. In doing so, they have to consider their family budget in the context of the needs of their own children.   This often leaves little to cover the cost of care for ageing parents. When an older person because of health, age, or emotional reasons cannot live alone or with family, an eldercare facility must be considered.

Finding an affordable senior facility with healthy design and timeless style that provides peace of mind with age-appropriate furniture and programs is not easy. It should be close to family, within the family budget, and accessible by family and friends. Check out the opportunities and make sure everyone is satisfied with the choice. Speak with the adult children of those who reside in the particular place and seek a reference. The more you learn about the place the easier it will be to make a choice. Normally, they will provide truthful answers to your questions. Once your questions are answered, make a final decision and discuss it with the family. Long Term Care (LTC) policy explanation is beyond the scope of this book. Always check with your insurance professionals and see if any of your policies cover LTC or extended care. If not, the family will have to assume the accountability.

Ageing vs. Alternative

No one should regret growing older. The alternative is premature death. Growing old is a privilege denied to many. Is ageing the real issue or do we just fail to understand the nature of ageing? Perhaps we should change the word or at least the normal perspective of the concept of ageing. Better wording could be maturing, growing older, advancing in years, or the accumulation of birthday celebrations over time. Ageing generally refers to a multidimensional process of physical, psychological, and social change. Perhaps having Birthday Celebrations is the problem; just celebrate the anniversary of your birth and honor your parents. This way the years seem not to count. At least one gains a different perspective on ageing.

Things Change with Age

At an annual check-up, a physician explained the pain on one side of a lady's body as the effect of ageing. She was adamant and said, "You missed that diagnosis doctor because this side is just as old as the hurting side, and it doesn't hurt." Age may be a factor contributing to the pain on one side, but doctors would be wise to explain it in a different way. However, the ageing process does change the physical appearance and this reduces self-confidence.   Ageing reduces one's strength for physical activity and this impacts the self-confidence of seniors. Weakened muscles, loss of hearing, worse eye sight, and recurring and/or constant pain causes a slow erosion of independence. This impacts the self-confidence of the elderly. One always fears the unknown. Always insist on the whole truth and nothing but the truth from caregivers and the medical community.

No Path Forward

Dealing only with the problems related to ageing, provides no path forward. The elderly must be guided to concentrate on the things that matter now: the things they can do. Surely, there will be a few problems and some aches and pains, but these can be managed by an understanding family or caregiver. Seniors must accept the changes and move forward with confidence. The path forward is based on confidence and knowledge.

Snapdragon Phase of Life

A snapdragon is a plant in the herb family that can be used for flavoring, food, medicine, or perfume. Snapdragons have flowers that appear in two forms: one develops outside the main bloom before it opens; the other delayed bloom is a showy "two-lip" blossom. These two blooms have caused some to see ageing as having a "snapdragon" phase. When it becomes difficult to bloom where you are planted because of premature intrusions that permit a counterproductive "two-lip talking head" to openly and constantly remind you of past problems, you have reached the "snapdragon" phase of life. When it becomes difficult to live a positive life because your head is filled with past problems, this "snapdragon" phase will cause some parts to snap and other parts to keep dragging you down and delaying your forward progress. Certainly, strong people make the same mistakes that weak ones do, but they admit them, learn from them, and move on with their life. Life is too short to walk around angry with an overload of problems: forgive, forget and move on and this could be the best part of your life.

Physical Activity

Participation in physically-appropriate activities will provide an opportunity for exercise and satisfy the need to keep doing things the elderly enjoy. Any physical activity, whether it is reading a book, sweating in the gym, hiking along a scenic trail, or playing a sport appropriate for their physical limitations, will boost the self-confidence in other aspects of life. Another example of ageing difficulties relate to an elderly individual who loves to read, but is suffering from sight loss. The best solution is to take them to a library that loans audio books. This becomes a double blessing: they get outside and are able to continue enjoying a good book. These are positive steps in the right direction.

Win or Lose

One example relates to sports. The young learn the rules of a given sport and their bodies are able to function within those boundaries; however, as they age the body does not respond the same as before and this causes injuries. It seems that muscles remember how to play the game, but the body is no longer able to reach and stretch and injuries occur. Seniors should not attempt to participate in the games they played in their youth. As one grows older, they must choose new sports activities that are within their physical capabilities. As they play age-appropriate games their self-confidence will improve. They can satisfy their desire to compete where they have a chance to win. Participation in a sport appropriate to their physical capabilities will provide good exercise where they win or not. This will strengthen their self-confidence.

Building Self-confidence

Self-confidence is the difference between feeling self-reliant and being overwhelmed or frightened about present circumstance or the foreseeable future. Some believe that perception is reality; that is, the way one actually feels about their existence. The way seniors feel about themselves, also has an enormous impact on how others see them. When the confidence is low, the self-assurance will be low. This will cause others to view the elderly as being insecure and unproductive. This view causes family or caregivers to view seniors as someone just waiting to die. With this attitude the sky is always filled with dark clouds and uncertainty. It doesn't have to be that way. When the factors that affect self-confidence are beyond the control of the individual, the family, or caregivers should encourage the elderly to do several things to improve self-confidence.

1. **Improve Appearance** --Buying cheap clothes just clutters the closet and does not improve attitude or appearance. It is not necessary to spend a lot of money, just buy quality items. After all, quality clothes stay in style longer and normally last longer. Wearing quality clothing improves self-confidence. The elderly should dress every day to face the world. No one

wants to appear lazy or sickly by lounging around in bedroom or house clothes. House clothes means no one is going anywhere.

2. Seniors are often more conscious of their physical appearance than one thinks. Dressed in bed or lounge clothing suggests that no one is coming to visit. When one doesn't look good it changes their feeling about themselves. The first step in building self-confidence is to see that the elderly are dressed neatly and ready to receive visitors or ready to walk out the front door into their field of dreams. Self-confidence is increased by a warm bath, clean, stylish clothes, and a smile from those around. Personal appearance is important to the elderly. If personal appearance is improved; self-confidence will increase.

3. **Work on Energy** – When one walks slowly without energy or purpose they appear old and sickly. Confident individuals walk quickly; they have places to go, things to do, and people to see. The elderly should be encouraged to walk a little faster; they will feel younger, stronger and more important. The message sent by body language and dress has a loud voice and is heard by everyone in the environment.

4. **Improve Posture** – Individuals with slumped shoulders and sluggish movement appear less confident. Encourage good posture among the elderly. When one stands up straight, keeps their head up, and makes eye contact with others, they make a positive impression. They automatically feel better, more alert and encouraged about their surroundings and relationships. Good posture improves both attitude and appearance. Good shoes are the foundation of posture and comfort all day. When even the little toe is uncomfortable, the whole body suffers fatigue.

5. **Make a Performance** – Seniors should take a seat up front in all meetings, not just because you can hear better, but to demonstrate real interest in the meeting.

The elderly should be encouraged to tell stories about their life. True tales about exciting events become a source of energy and excitement for the storyteller and the hearer. Writing and/or reciting a poem, singing a song, playing an instrument, dancing a jig, or participating in a fun game will build self-confidence. Speaking up in a group discussion and sharing one's knowledge and experience improves a sense of self-worth. Personal performance is always a good boost for seniors.

6. **Show Appreciation** – When one concentrates on something positive and shows appreciation or demonstrates gratitude, their self-confidence grows. If the elderly are allowed to dwell on their weakness, past failures, or focus on just what they want, it breeds discouragement and creates reasons why they can no longer do the things that made them happy. However, if one practices being grateful for what they have now rather than complaining or comparing the present with the past, their happiness and self-confidence will increase.

7. **Seek Activity** – Remaining active is important to self-worth and self-image. Personal appearance and physical fitness have good impact on self-esteem. Physical exercise or a work out with a group will bring energy and the feeling of a finished task." This becomes a major accomplishment for seniors and is vital to self-confidence. Of course, all activity must be age-appropriate. To attempt a physical activity and fail because of a lack of strength or agility can damage self-confidence. All physical activity must be adjusted to age and abilities. Activity should produce positive momentum for the rest of the day and produce a positive view of the future.

8. **Focus on Others** – A first step toward self-confidence is to compliment others. Look for reasons to express approval and offer praise for the work or accomplishments of others. The cook should be

complimented for a good meal. The hair-dresser or barber should be thanked for a good job. The individual who cleans the house, washes the dishes, makes the beds, waters the flowers or cuts the grass, deserve a compliment. The habit of expressing approval is not the same as flattery; that is, giving excessive compliments, but praising others can break a cycle of negativity that often becomes a part of the ageing process. Avoid gossip and never engage in backstabbing, but always show approval of others and more self-confidence will be a beneficial result.

Paint Things Green

Color psychology is more important than first reported. You may have painted the town "red" when you were young, but now you are at a different stage in life. Avoid being sad and blue. You have a different brush, a new canvas, and should use a different paint: the recommended color is "green." Your lifestyle should be peaceful, calm, and green. Why green? The color green usually represents growth and promise. When one sees a green leaf on a tree in the springtime, it is the evidence of life and the promise of fruit. The environmentalists keep telling us "Go Green!" For the elderly going green means more than a walk in the park or drinking a cup of green tea; it has to do with a positive mental attitude that brings peace and calm to life's troubling situations.

The "Green Age"

The senior years could be called the "green age," because as long as you live, you are growing in understanding, knowledge, and wisdom. You may not be growing taller, but you are enlarging at the middle and the bottom. All you have learned in the past has prepared you for this time. You must gain a different perspective of yourself; you are changing with age. All of life before prepared you for this phase of life; this phase is important and you are a person of value.   You may not walk as fast, or act as quickly, but your knowledge and expertise have increased in value. Share it with anyone who will listen. If individuals will not listen, turn up the charm and share what you know with the group. Others will be interested. Perhaps they will share too and you will learn more.

Think Green!

In a bouquet of flowers, although the blooms are colorful it was a green stem that supported the growth of the beautiful colors. When one discovers the symbolism of color, the pigment between blue and yellow in the spectrum is green. It is the color of grass or emeralds and represents fresh value, youth, and new life; it is the color of nature, fertility, and life. Green symbolizes self-respect and well-being. It is the color of spring, the nature of growing things; it speaks of renewal and rebirth. Green demonstrates life and promises fruit. The color green renews and restores depleted energy. Think green! When one thinks of a "green kid" it is because the child is growing and does not relate to ignorance. Ageing can become a browning time and needs the renewal of springtime, the greening of the forest and the fields, the blooming of colorful flowers, the chirpings of birds, the hopping of rabbits, to demonstrate renewal and growth. Ageing has a Silver Lining; it is a sign of hope in an unfortunate situation; a bright prospect for the future.

Primary Concerns

One elderly gentleman speaking to friends said, "I think I am entering some 'metallic' period of life: my hair is gray, there is gold in my teeth, I have steel toed shoes, and it seems there is lead in my pants. How older people deal with the inevitable problems of ageing should be a primary concern of every member of the family.   There is a growing uneasiness about how the elderly see the world and themselves. The way seniors are treated and valued speaks to the morality of the society. Anxieties exist among the elderly about health and income issues. Normal health matters relate to less hearing, weakened eyesight, and diminished memory, and the ever-present probability of a fall or serious illness.   However, more people are entering old age with relatively good health due to better medical care and nutrition and most of the elderly learn to adapt to the limitations imposed by ageing problems. In general, the health of present seniors is better than previous generations. This will probably improve still further as more people grow up with a better diet and receive better medical care throughout their lives. In most industrial societies, the high cost of treating chronic illness has been partially assumed by insurance and national health plans. A primary concern is the cost of care and housing for the senior population and apprehension about longevity.

Income and Economic Wellbeing

A *major problem* of seniors is income and economic well-being. Because most of the elderly are no longer in the labor force, some form of income maintenance is necessary. Industrial societies have developed systems of pensions and social benefits. Although the income of retired people is about half that of the working public, most manage to maintain themselves a bit above the poverty level. In most areas, women and other minorities continue to have support issues. Because of the higher death rate for men than for women, many widows are left to fend for themselves. Women among the elderly have the greatest needs. Who will care for the ageing mothers and widows?

Living Arrangements

Most seniors prefer independent living in their own home. Many elderly live with an adult child, and some are in adult retirement centers or eldercare housing, but all wish to remain within a few hours of children or relatives. Those with serious health problems require assisted living situations or nursing care facilities. Only a few elderly parents are neglected by their children. Nonetheless, there comes a time when both a personal and a family decision must be made as to where the elderly will spend their last years. It is never wise to delay decisions about where seniors will live during the last decades of life.

No Room for Indecisiveness

Stop wavering and become resolute, there is no room in the ageing process for indecisiveness or frustration about growing older; it is inevitable. The anxiety appears when one is indecisive or unclear about the reality of advancing age.

Knowledge can relieve the apprehension and produce a Silver Lining to the clouds that normally hover over the elderly. Age is a single frame in a color photograph. It contains thousands of colors and the ability to see the various values depends on clear and enlarged thinking about the issue at hand. Many actually enjoy the slowdown and having time for the long "honey-do list" that had to wait for the hustle and bustle to taper off. Most seniors appreciate and prefer the quietness of home to the activity and noisy surroundings at the workplace.

Age as a Snap Shot

The basic problem is that most seniors refuse to develop a larger view of life and see age as a simple snap shot that does not clearly develop or show the future. The snap shot only reveals what existed at the moment and does not provide a glimpse into the future. Viewing the future with confidence can enlarge the picture and enable one to see more clearly the surroundings. This should diminish the discouragement that comes with seeing the thinning hair, wrinkles and blemishes of age. When one thinks backward from the snap shot with memories of the past it only produces a "negative" perspective. Looking forward to a current photograph, you may want to destroy that negative, too. Sadly, on January 8, 2014, I saw an aged picture of Elvis Presley on the Internet. On his birthday, someone had aged a photograph to how Elvis would look at 78; it was sad and shocking, but realistic.

No you will never again look the same as you did at 21 or 35, but you have improved in many ways; the bright light of the inner you still shines. The view must always be forward in spite of an ageing body, you are better than you ever were. The future is always brighter when you face reality and open your eyes and see a loving family and old friends close by your side. Things are not the same; they are better than ever with grandchildren and/or old friends around. After all, your friends look old, too. Their memory sees you as young and vibrant. You may look better than they remember. Sometimes a few gray hairs adds a certain dignity and maturity to appearance that was not present in younger days.

Nuggets of Wisdom

Certainly there are snap shot memories of the past that can be nuggets of wisdom that inspire and encourage the elderly. The memory of a small, growing child causes one to see the potential for growth and prospects for the future. A photograph taken of a family vacation can cause one to concentrate on the growth and development of the family and their accomplishments. Do not spend one moment thinking about the negative aspects of the past, because each life is filled with undesirable moments. These, however, can be obscured by the good memories of family and friends. Emphasizing the positive and eliminating the negative can produce a Silver Lining to even a clouded memory. With a positive perspective, the future can be filled with sunshine.

Personal Perspective

Everyone has a personal perspective based on their self-image. A positive image and self-worth both come from the good inside; not what others see or think. A strong sense of self-worth can enable one to assert the right to be whom and what they expect of themselves. This is your personal truth; what you believe about yourself. This private photograph of your inner self should be enlarged until you can clearly see all the colors, shades and tones. This is where your true character emerges and your positive qualities manifest themselves. There is much more to you and your past than a few bad memories. Sure each life has some bitter roots, but similar to a fruit tree you can compensate, overcome and produce positive fruit that will grow and ripen in the sunshine. Fruit is always on new growth after the tree was watered by the rain. Let the rainy days produce positive fruit in the sunshine of your daily life.

Discard Bad Memories

What if you find bad pictures (photos) in your memory? Do you not normally discard old pictures that remind you of bad times? Have you not torn a photograph in half to remove the image of an old flame that burned out long ago? Then, you must do that with negative memories and preserve only the positive ones. The senior memory of old photographs also includes the knowledge that there were "negatives" of these pictures. Although it is difficult to forget something when it is known, it's kind of like trying to unsnap a photo or un-ring a bell. Yet, you can discard the bad photos and destroy the negatives associated with them. Then look in a mirror and snap a fresh picture of the new you. You have personal worth and value. You are more than the sum total of your past or body parts; you are what you have become. Look at the new snap shot and say:

This is who I am now,
I renounce the former me and the
bad memories associated with my old self.
From this day forward, I will remember only this
new 'make over' of myself.

This will be who I am as I walk
confidently into the future.
The rest of my life will be
the best of my life.

Take Positive Action

Positive action is the key to seeing the Silver Lining among the clouds that hang over the past. The Silver Lining means the sun is shining above and soon the clouds will disappear and the bright light will shine on your personal path forward. This positive mindset will bring peace and happiness to each forward step of the journey. The good life is not a dream; it is a goal. The difference between a dream and a goal is that you can create an agenda for a goal, a step by step way to reach the desired result. Dreams vanish into thin air, but positive steps toward a goal produce a sense of real satisfaction and accomplishment. Having a goal will give you a reason to wake up and start a new day with excitement. Choose to live a positive lifestyle. Otherwise, your days will be filled with problems and disappointment. You will have a meaningful existence only if you choose to live a positive way of life. Do not permit others to write the last chapters of your life. Choose the positive path forward and enjoy each day and decade of the journey. The day may be long, but you have many miles to go before sundown. Enjoy the journey.

Social Support and Control

Many have examined the factors concerning the coping skills of seniors; such as, social support, religion, active engagement with life and the level of confidence that individuals have control over their personal lives. These factors reveal their ability to cope with stressful events of daily life. Social support and personal control over lifestyle are possibly the two most important factors that predict well-being, bad health and ultimately death in adults. Other factors that may link to well-being and quality of life include social relationships and a peaceful and wholesome environment in which to live.

Faith and Cultural Systems

Personal faith and cultural systems, including religion, appear to be important factors in coping with the demands of later life. These become more evident as one faces the long good bye with family and friends. The expression of faith and cultural systems, in the broadest sense, refers to many aspects of religious and traditional activity, personal dedication and belief expressed in the life of an individual. Participation in formal and organized religious activities may decline among the elderly, but normally faith is expressed through personal and private prayers and meditation. Participation in the formal side of religion may decrease, but principles and moral values are multidimensional variables and will continue to be practiced in a moral lifestyle and informally in daily expressions of confidence in the future and the afterlife. Personal faith and a connection to a cultural system are vital to mental, physical, and spiritual health during the ageing process.

Individual Control of Health

It has become obvious that health issues among seniors are mostly in the hands of the individual. Without discipline and willpower that controls diet and produces exercise, the elderly will continue to suffer preventable maladies. All individuals past the age of 40 must take control of their own health. One cannot depend on pills, shots and medical concoctions prescribed by physicians to produce cures or terminate disease, disorders, or ailments. This reminds me of a young man psychologically disturbed over the death of his father and was placed in a juvenile care facility. After a few days of rest and counseling, his mother and a friend were permitted to visit. During the visit, the counselor asked the young man, "What are we going to do about this temper?" The response "Can't you give me a shot for that?" When the counselor shared that there was no shot for temper, the young man replied, "I know there is because they gave my dog a shot for his temper." The counselor explained, "There is a big difference in human 'temper' and canine 'distemper'." Distemper in a dog is caused by a virus similar to the one that causes measles in people, while human temper is a state of mind. Also, there are big differences in physical and psychological maladies.

The maladies of age are best prevented. The old adage, "An ounce of prevention is worth a pound of cure" should be taken into account by seniors who sincerely want to enjoy the last decade of life. Not all, but many of the medical and physical woes of age, can be prevented or at least lessened; consequently, the elderly must see their personal culpability for some of their age-related suffering. A positive personal lifestyle is required to assure better health. Society must not permit seniors to vegetate and exist in monotony and inactivity. If the old saying "Once a man; twice a child" is true, then the last years of life should be filled with the laughter of a child. This does not mean that seniors are "childish" but just as children do, seniors have the potential for growth and joy.

Life is a Brief Journey

Life is short from the start; a brief journey through time and space. You may never reach all the high goals established for your life, but you can enjoy the journey anyway. Long-ranged planning is designed to keep you from becoming discouraged with short-term problems. After all, the end is not what you seek; it is the pleasure of the journey that brings joy and excitement. It is similar to Christmas ...when it's over... it's over and the credit cards are due. Enjoy the journey, each and every moment along the way. Each new day is a divine gift, rejoice and be glad the next twenty-four hours. Each day may have a few bumps and rocks in the road, but don't stumble or pick up and carry the rocks into tomorrow. Let each day count for the good. Life is similar to a long trip, when you arrive at the final destination you will be weary and need a long rest. Forget the question, "Are we there yet?" The excitement of living is the daily journey forward with all the beautiful scenes along the way. When you get there…you are just **there**! Often "there" means nowhere else to go….! Don't permit the past or "there" to define your present happiness. The present is not the end of the journey; it is just a passing day, there is always tomorrow. Have a night's rest, enjoy living but don't dwell on the chronological aspects of life. After all, "age" is a state of mind anyway. A nourishing diet and a little exercise can become a Silver Lining to the difficulties of the journey.

Life is About the Future

Life itself is about the future, not the past. Birth, growing up, courtship, marriage, children, education, work, and religion are all about the future. The forward aspects of the journey matters more than the beginning or even the recurring problems along the way. Moving the human cargo forward is essential to all aspects of health.   Destinations are important, but the journey is where the excitement is experienced. In the sale of real estate, the operative word is "location," but in life's journey it is clearly the "process" that brings peace and joy. A snapshot of where you are may not please you, but enjoy the days ahead anyway. This is what matters. The pursuit of happiness is the reality of pleasure, not the destination. Planning the family vacation and the joy of getting there were often more exciting than being "there." Yet, the future destination determines the direction of the journey and becomes guidance for the forward steps.   In fact, a good nutritious meal can make one forget their age and even some problems of the past.   A meal is more about connectedness than it is about food. Eating food you enjoy can bring to mind good memories of grandparents, parents, old friends, and even places you visited with family. Food can enhance your lifestyle.

DREAMS VS. GOALS

4

LEARNING

ABOUT NUTRITION AND LIFESTYLE

Obsession about Longevity

Ponce de Leon supposedly discovered a Fountain of Youth in Florida. Most believe this to be a myth, because drinking the water from this mystical fountain, never extended the life of anyone beyond their normal years. Juan Ponce de Leon himself (if he drank the water) died in the summer of 1521 at the age of 47. Through the past decades many native remedies, restorative elixirs and "snake-oil potions" were concocted, sold, tried and failed. Yet, in recent years, the fairytale of longevity has offered false hope that discoveries will be made to reverse the ageing process and allow people to live a longer life in good health. It is estimated that some with proper diet, exercise and medical discoveries will have a few extra birthdays. The obsession about finding the secret to longevity of life continues. Meanwhile, everyone must prepare for the last decades of life.

Sound and Rational Thinking

According to Harvard Medical School, prescription medications that could prevent age-related illnesses might be marketed in a few years. Yet, illness is not the only barrier to longevity. If the pharmaceutical company researchers successfully formulate a longevity pill, it will be expensive. In Elizabethan times, people were told that nutmeg could ward off the plague; the price of nutmeg skyrocketed beyond the reach of the average family. Harvard is looking at the compound found in the skin of red grapes that might protect the body from ageing. This will only advance the obsession about longevity. If the chemical pathway that activates a protein related to health and longevity is discovered, the price would be beyond the budget of most families. This means the true path to eldercare and health during the ageing process remains in the hands of the individual and their family. Certainly, a proper diet, exercise and a positive mental attitude can bring perspective and reality to longevity, but it must include sound and rational thinking about the rate of ageing and the process of preparing for the later decades of life. Presently there are no medical solutions to the multiple problems of ageing.

Rate of Ageing

Not everyone ages in the same way. There is a variety of intrinsic and extrinsic elements that affect the rate of ageing. Ageing issues include genetic factors and heredity that are foundational to the ageing process. It is personal behavior, the environment, and the stress and strain of modern life that cause illness, injuries, and emotional stress. These are contributing factors to illness and the early demise of many.

State of Ageing

In biology, *senescence* is the state or process of ageing. Between the ages of 20 and 35, humans have almost perfect renewal that lessens the intensity of the ageing process. After age 40, most individuals are less able to respond to stress, and this decreases the ability to maintain internal stability and increases the risk of disease. This series of irreversible changes predictably ends in lingering disability and death. As research isolates genes that influence ageing and develops a usable medical application, the process of ageing may become treatable. Until then, ageing human beings must all plan for the final decades of life. To date no one has found the Fountain of Youth or developed a Methuselah pill.

Dietary Restriction

Lifespan research has determined that diet restriction may affect the longevity of some lower animals and a few primates. The big question is simply, "Will this ever be extended beyond primates, such as the Rhesus monkeys studied by the U.S. National Institute of Health? Since the increase in lifespan for monkeys was only notable when the caloric restriction was started early in life, it cannot be generalized to the human population. Tragically, this is not a Silver Lining for longevity, because poor dietary habits during childhood and early adulthood already established many aspects of the undernourished and overweight lifestyle existing in older adults.

Caloric Restriction

Some research in caloric restriction of 30–50% less than the subject would normally consume, did increase the lifespan, but the provision was clear the diet must maintain proper nutrients. There were no data available as to the energy or productivity of subjects with the restrictive diet. However, specific caloric restriction on prisoners of war left decimated individuals and the denial of food in genocidal societies resulted in massive deaths. There is a story of an old farmer that grew tired of feeding an old mule that could no longer work. He decided to try to gradually cut back on his normal feeding. The tragic end of the old mule was shared with a neighbor, "About the time I got him weaned from food, he died!" It is certain that restriction of caloric intake would have destructive results on the elderly. A balanced and nutritious diet is necessary for physical and mental health for all age groups. Certainly, cut backs in the family food budget, is not an answer to the needs of the elderly.

Dreams vs. Goals

Some see no difference in a dream and a goal. It is difficult to write an agenda for a dream, but when one thinks realistically about the life of an elderly person, perhaps an agenda is actually possible. Processing any aspect of life is to see it in parts or segments that are connected and together form a whole. Each area of life requires productive behavior and adequate production requires work without loss or waste. This means one must balance the basic elements of achievements in each segment of life. When it comes to living a productive life as a senior citizen, a learned sage, or a person with expertise, one needs a plan. If you know a person who has lived a long life and desires to speculate about the present and the future, they should follow some planned steps.

Turn Dreams into a Plan

To fulfill the expectations of any phase of life, one must have more than a personal DREAM. A specific plan that deals with [**D**iet-**R**est-**E**xercise-**A**ccomplishment-**M**edication] is crucial. Follow your **D. R. E. A. M. on**ly if you have a plan that includes a healthy diet; proper rest, regular exercise, specific work and accomplishment, and the use of prescribed medication. This can produce a positive lifestyle regardless of age or circumstance.

D— Follow a healthy **DIET;**

R— Arrange for adequate **REST;**

E— Maintain regular **EXERCISE;**

A— Schedule specific **ACCOMPLISHMENT;**

M— Remember prescribed **MEDICATION.**

Proper Diet Required

Many of the elderly are malnourished either by overeating or by under consumption of nutritious foods. As people age the need for calories decreases, while the need for nutrients normally increases. This becomes a challenge for families with seniors and eldercare facilities. A healthy diet for seniors was dealt with constructively by the British Columbia Ministry of Health Services (Canada). (See **Appendix Three**) An excellent 214 page handbook, *Healthy Eating for Seniors,* is available for free download at their Internet site: http://www.healthlinkbc.ca/pdf/HEFS_english.pdf.   It is a large file and maybe a slow download, but it is an excellent guide for the nourishment and care for seniors. The download and use of this document is worth your time. It can be of great assistance to eldercare facilities and families with seniors living at home. This excerpt is from the Foreword:

> *The saying, "You are what you eat," is true. A healthy diet provides the ingredients to build and*

*repair bones and tissues and keep the complex
workings of the human body functioning optimally.
It also provides the mental and physical energy
necessary for daily life – work, recreation,
relationships and time with family. It is clear that
a healthy diet also protects us from infectious
illnesses and chronic diseases so that we may age
with a minimum of ill health, pain and disability.*

— From the Foreword, Healthy Eating for Seniors

Healthy Eating

For the elderly, the diet should follow the principles of a healthy balanced diet. The sense of taste and smell decline with age, which can make food seem less appetizing. Using different colors and shapes in cooking can stimulate the senses and add to eating enjoyment. The addition of herbs and spices can also make food more interesting. An increase in starchy, fiber-providing foods and a reduction in fatty and sugary foods are likely to be most beneficial, particularly if individuals are overweight. However, a low-fat, high-fiber diet is not appropriate for all elderly people, especially those with repeated infections, generally poor health or a poor appetite. Quality health may be improved by a diet that includes soluble fiber found in beans, oatmeal, and many fruits and vegetables. Adding whole grains, daily exercise, and meditation to relax and reduce stress may also increase the quality of life. Drinking plenty of water is essential to good health. If drinking a sufficient quantity of water becomes a bore, wake it up by adding a little fruit juice. Put limits on salt, sugar, and other savory items to balance your diet.

It is important that older people choose a nutrient rich diet, high in foods providing protein, vitamins and minerals such as milk and dairy products, meat, eggs, fish, bread, cereals, and fruit and vegetables. A varied diet will also help to ensure adequate nutritional intake. Snacks can be an important part of the diet in older age groups, particularly for those unable to cope with large meals at one sitting. Dairy products such as milk provide an excellent way to furnish a nutrient rich snack along with fluid for individuals who are struggling to meet the daily requirements.

Make Dietary Changes Slowly

Good nutrition does not come from random, undisciplined eating; it is never here today and gone tomorrow. In fact, it is part of a healthy lifestyle that is adopted for years to come. Perhaps one should see **"DIET"** as something you "<u>D</u>o <u>I</u>t <u>E</u>ach <u>T</u>ime" you eat. To eat healthier, begin with small steps, and make one change at a time. For example, you could take the salt shaker off the table or just decrease salt intake slowly and allow your appetite to adjust. Also, you could switch to whole-grain bread, seafood, or more vegetables and fruits with each meal. Work your taste buds; it may take several trials to develop a taste for the flavor of new foods.

Seniors Living at Home

It is a good idea for older people living alone or with family to keep an emergency store of some basic foods items for times when it is difficult to get to the store. Useful stored items may include:

- Milk, for example, long-life, evaporated, dried milk and tinned milky puddings.
- Canned meat and fish e.g. tins of corned beef, stewed meats, ham, sardines, salmon, and tuna.
- Tinned fruit and vegetables e.g. tinned peaches, baked beans, sweet corn, peas, and tomatoes.
- Dried fruit.
- Breakfast cereals or porridge oats.
- Crackers, biscuits, crisp bread and oatcakes (in an airtight tin).
- Rice and pasta.
- Soups (canned and packet).
- Drinks e.g. cocoa, malted milk, long-life fruit juice, tea and coffee and meal replacement drinks.
- Other: stock cubes, gravy, honey, jam, peanut butter, pickles and sauces.

Physical Activity and Calories

A healthy weight can be controlled by balancing calories with activity. Simple math: the less activity the fewer calories.

Extra weight for the elderly can increase the risk of diseases; such as, Type 2 diabetes, heart disease, and joint problems. Eating more calories than your activity requires will lead to extra "pounds." As one ages and becomes less active physically, they will need fewer calories to maintain the same weight. Choosing nutrition over calories is the answer.

Foods Affect Digestion

The choice of foods will affect digestion; for instance, insufficient fiber and/or fluids may cause constipation. More whole-grain foods with fiber, fruits and vegetables combined with more water will assist with regularity. If the Chinese are correct that proper circulation and elimination of waste from the body is the key to health, then a proper diet is required to maintain regularity. One of the most common digestive complaints is constipation. It may be a severe or lingering condition, but it is a symptom rather than a disease and can be corrected by diet and exercise.

Health Controlled by Nutrients

Calories are a way to measure the energy obtained from food. A proper diet may enable energy levels to meet the needs of activity. Food is fuel for the body, not entertainment or a "treat" for an uneventful or boring life. The need for calories depends on age, gender, height/weight, and the level of activity. A well-planned, balanced, and nutritional eating plan can produce good and healthy benefits. A proper diet may reduce the risk of heart disease, stroke, diabetes, bone loss, some cancers, and conditions that reduce red blood cells that provide oxygen to body tissues. Even for those who already have a lingering disease, eating well and regular physical activity may assist in managing your health. A healthy diet provides the nutrients needed to keep muscles, bones, organs, and other body parts healthy through a lifespan. The required nutrients include vitamins, minerals, protein, carbohydrates, some fats, and water. A good diet is not complicated; it is sophisticated. Once you understand and follow the rules, a nutritious diet becomes easy to follow.

Nutrition should be Easy

Such changes may be easier than one thinks, even on a limited budget. If you need help getting groceries, instruct others about the foods you need and the ones to avoid for your health. If the food is not in the cupboard, you will not be tempted to eat it. The beginning of a healthy diet and lifestyle can start now regardless of age. A proper diet can assist everyone to stay healthy and live a more fulfilling and independent life. This is especially true for the elderly. Those taking prescription medicines should check with their physician or a registered dietitian about foods that could interact negatively with the medicine. Proper nutrition can cause anyone to look and feel better. A healthy person normally looks better to others.

Manage Meds Properly

Most seniors take multiple medications. At times they have prescriptions from different physicians. Since some drugs and medicines interact dangerously with others, it is important that a primary doctor manage all medication. This means the primary physician must review all prescriptions, including over-the-counter drugs and supplements. One medical person should make sure that each drug, supplement, and prescription is appropriate for the present state of health and does not interact with negatively with another. Also, no one should stop taking a prescription medication without their primary care person being fully aware. Due to perceived side effects, the elderly may be tempted to stop taking a particular medication. The sudden withdrawal from some drugs and medications can cause harm. This should be done only with the knowledge of the person who manages all personal medication.

Stuck in 1950

Whether it is nutrition, exercise, or technology, family members and caregivers must not permit seniors to get stuck in 1950. Those days have gone the way of the horse and buggy. Advancing new technology waits for no one. Those who delay and fail to learn to function with new things will be left behind. A caring thing one can do for an older person is to provide them with the know-how to function with modern technology. New and fresh ways to do things, especially communication, can bring both peace and productivity to seniors. They may have resisted their first ride on an airplane, the push button telephone, the automatic appliances, and other gadgets, but to deny seniors the functional use of technology will further complicate their life and care. After all it is as simple as pushing a few buttons. The elderly can still learn new things and modern technology can improve their health and safety. Cell phone technology can be both a comfort and a joy to a lonely senior. By carrying a cell phone on their person, a senior feels both safe and connected.

"Opportunity" still Exploring

If the Rover space vehicle, named "Opportunity", was still exploring Mars after a decade, surely the elderly can learn to push a few new buttons. This space vehicle was launched about 10 years ago, (*that's a lot of dog years according to Veterinarian research -- 10 dog years is 62 human years*) and "Opportunity" is still functioning all alone in outer space.   Yes, it has some wear and tear and one of its six wheels and two instruments stopped working long ago. The Rover's flash memory sometimes suffers a senior moment and some of its gears and joints are stiff, yet it still has value and is working under extreme conditions. The seniors of society have value and need modern technology to make their communication easier and more rewarding for themselves and others. Regardless of age or aches and pains, most seniors can still use some modern technology (computers, cell phone, medical alert devices, etc.) to increase their security and prompt personal communications.

Benefit from New Technology

Many of the elderly have resisted the use of advance technology available to improve communication with family and friends. The use of a personal laptop, the convenience of a cell phone, and learning the advantage of texting or the security of a medical alert device, can brighten the day of one who feels alone. If the very young can push the buttons on a video game and master the texting process on a cell phone, the elderly can benefit from learning and using the new technology. It would be a pleasant surprise for the elderly to get an email from a grandchild or a text message from family or an old friend. All connections with others are beneficial for seniors.

Generational Conversations

Although most of the elderly have resisted modern technology, the best way for them to enjoy life now is to remain current with new equipment and learn to operate the modern gadgets or what some seniors call new "thingamajigs or whatchamacallits." As the whole world embraces the pairing of technology with human needs, seniors must not be left out of the loop. Adequate and prompt interaction with new technology remains crucial to the well-being of seniors. Modern technology can enable continued generational conversations with the extended family and old friends during the ageing process. This increases the sense of companionship and connectedness and enables seniors to cope with social isolation.

5

Contending
with Social Isolation

Seniors Risk Isolation

The ageing population, as a group, are at risk of social isolation. They are no longer gainfully employed and have outlived many of their friends. The loss of close family members increases the loneliness. Financial considerations and common health issues restrict their activities and a feeling of separation normally increases as one ages. Delayed getting in touch with an elderly family member or ageing friends, may cause the loss of critical generational interaction and exchanges with the elderly. The loss of wisdom and true life experiences would be irreplaceable and heartbreaking for all concerned.

Social Isolation

When one is suffering an extended illness, it appears that visits from friends and family may actually help ward off inflammation. Could it be that social contacts are good medicine? Ancient sacred writings declared, "Laughter does good like a medicine." Social isolation creates stress and activates an inflammatory response and weakens several body systems. Of course, quality sleep is a restorative process to facilitate better health but without the frequent visits of family and friends most of medicine and nutrition are of less value. The sick and elderly need regular contact with family and friends. Aloneness can complicate their condition. Even a brief visit or a phone call can be beneficial.

Dealing with Loss

The senior community constantly deals with the loss of family and dear friends. This causes insecurity and weakens self-confidence. Loss produces mistrust of one's own judgment, ability, strength, and capacity to function. Helping seniors make new friends and getting them involved with physical and social activities will greatly improve their self-confidence and health. Seniors are human beings and need connections and compliments from close family and valued friends. To hear "You're looking good, today!" can lift the spirits of a senior, even if it is just a social statement.

Grief and Depression Associated

Grief and depression appear to be associated especially among the elderly who have experienced a significant loss. A gloomy situation may normally be turned into a place of love, light, and laughter by a thoughtful compassionate caregiver, but grief is a normal response to loss. When an elderly person suffers from extended grief and it develops into depression their medications alone may not be sufficient to provide relief. Such grief can impact the whole emotional life and create hopeless and worthless feelings. The elderly feel loss when they become separated from loved ones. The loss of a position, income or any major change in life; such as, retiring or moving into new living space can create grief and ultimately depression. The loss of a spouse or a child can seriously complicate the health and well-being of anyone, but seniors are most vulnerable to such a personal loss.

Coping Mechanisms

Healthy people with good coping mechanisms are able to manage loss and still maintain the reality of daily responsibilities. When grief is acknowledged and allowed adequate healing time, the normal pattern of recovery seems to be sufficient. Others without coping skills or quality support continue until grief turns into deep depression. This pattern becomes more harmful as age increases. When normal grief turns into depression, seniors generally need professional treatment to deal with depression.

Grief and Depression Controversy

Normal grief and deep depression are a source of controversy. Most clinicians find it difficult to unscramble grief and depression; in fact, normal grief is not a disorder, but deep depression is a disorder and requires medical treatment. Significant research by Paula J. Clayton (1970's) demonstrated that sadness, tearfulness, sleep disturbance, decreased socialization, and appetite loss are witnessed in both normal grief and major depression. A person with prolonged depression sees people and their surroundings through dark glasses and will continue to live under dark clouds through rainy days without treatment. It becomes clear that care-givers of the elderly must refer individual with prolonged grief or depression for medical assistance. Normally, deep depression cannot be handled by family and friends. Professional assistance is needed in most cases.

Timeless Treasures

The memories of the elderly are a timeless treasure passed to the young in brief magical moments. It is the old who bring richness and meaning to the life of the young. If you ask almost anyone, who had the greatest influence on your life, they will share mostly older folks: a grandparent, an old uncle or aunt, an elderly teacher, a senior minister, a retired neighbor, or an elder statesman. There are countless ways to experience the wisdom and experience of the elderly, but the simplest is to just listen. As a good listener you get more from the magic moments spent with an elderly relative or friend. Always remember, it is all about them. Fill them in quickly on your news, then sit back and listen and learn from their stories and be inspired to live a fruitful and eventful life yourself. The good is shared freely while seniors tread softly through former fields of conflict. Don't ask questions, they will tell you what they want you to know. Just listen and the visit can be enchanting. Don't get stuck in a rut. If you delay getting in touch with an elderly family member or senior friends, you may forever lose irreplaceable and valued experiences. If an elderly member of the family or a close friend has moved to some type of eldercare facility, you must understand that your personal relationship has drastically changed. When seniors cannot live independently and perform adequate self-care, generational communication becomes more difficult. It takes lots of extra effort by both parties.

Healthy Relationships

Everyone deserves to be secure and have healthy relationships. Research suggested that a lack of companionship is a great challenge for all adults, especially for the elderly. Not only must seniors eat nutritiously, they must stay connected socially. A family-type mealtime could be part of the answer to this misfortune. Family members must understand the value of senior connectedness with family and friends. When seniors eat alone or with strangers, they feel a sense of isolation. Companionship makes a valuable contribution to better nutrition and healthy ageing. We all remember mama's cooking and the enjoyment of fellowship around a family meal. This is one of the most missed areas of a senior's life. Family and friends must find ways to meet this need. It may be different with each person, but the effort is worth the benefits.

Connectedness

The feeling of being connected to family and friends is worth the effort to make modern technology available to the elderly. As one lives longer or feels they are home alone during the day, or have moved to an eldercare facility, it is important to maintain a loving connection with them. When handwritten letters and cards become harder, the use of technology could be an answer to improved contact with seniors. The use of modern technology is a simple tool for improving communication between the generations. Regular communication in person and through media, honors relationships and enables an improved quality of life for the elderly.

Effective Communications

More effective communication with the elderly may occur when attention is paid to certain aspects of ageing. Ageing causes decline in some physical abilities that affect communication. Also, there are illnesses that make communication more difficult. The loss of hearing makes it harder to clearly understand, be patient and speak more plainly. Face to face is the best way to speak to seniors and always avoid talking while you eat. If hearing hinders telephone use or watching television, consider buying a listening device. Diminished vision can further complicate communication. Older folk often have a weaker voice that makes it harder to understand what is said. And of course there is always some memory loss as people age. Remember the senior is the patient, but you have to "be patient" with their limitations.

Patience is a Virtue

Always exercise patience when dealing with the elderly. Allow the elderly to reminisce. Because a senior's life experience is very different than yours or a caregiver's, it is vital to permit the elderly to express their thoughts and feelings in their own words. Respect the elderly person's background, knowledge, and values even if you disagree. Their losses include the death of family and friends, illnesses, the lack of productive work, or just the ageing process that produces sadness. The elderly need to grieve, be patient and listen. Grieving becomes a release valve and often eliminates additional problems. When the elderly feel that others do not understand their feelings, it complicates the exchange of information. Listening to an elderly person express their problems is a common kindness that should be freely shared. In fact, listening is a form of touching and can be most helpful to the elderly.

Mealtime Is a Challenge

Meals are not just about food; mealtime is a social event about sharing and connecting with others. Those seniors who live alone or in an eldercare facility soon discover that mealtime is a challenge. Not only the menu or preparation, but the aloneness creates a sense of separation from family and friends. Even in the best senior facility, mealtime always produces the emotion of loneliness. Most seniors readily declare that having good companionship makes mealtime

more satisfying. However, residents in a senior facility
are not "family" regardless of how hard the staff tries to
create attachment and inclusion. The elderly still need the
companionship of blood-relatives and lifelong friends. This is a
major difficulty with the later years of life and could be partially
solved if family and friends "made time" and did not live so far
away.   When family and friends share a meal with the elderly,
they are making a significant contribution to their health and
wellbeing.

Social Contact

Most senior facilities permit family and friends to initiate
social contact with the residents. Meeting with or taking
a senior for a family-type meal or a meal with friends in a
restaurant is a step in the right direction. Mealtime is a good
place for seniors to stay connected socially. Restaurants are
O.K., but eating a meal with family or friends in their home is
a welcomed event.   A home-cooked meal is always preferred
to the institutional menu. Even the sharing of a family favorite
dish with a senior is a beautiful thing. A good meal shared is
twice as nice.

Taste Buds Remember

Recently, two elderly members of an extended family
were invited to a Sunday dinner. The lady of the house made
a special effort to make a certain kind of bread normally eaten
by the guest's father and special sugar cookies similar to
what their mother made as they were growing up. When one
reached for the bread and tasted it, he remarked, "This is just
like Papa's!" At the close of the meal the sugar cookies were
passed around. The other elderly guest took a bite of a cookie
and exclaimed, "This taste just like Mama's sugar cookies."
Well enough said about good memories and taste buds.

The Void of Aloneness

When a senior feels isolated, it aggravates larger and
more comprehensive issues relative to challenges they
encounter as part of the ageing process. When seniors live
alone or even with family members that are away all day,
they feel alone. Television and music may help in such a

situation, but a pet (cat or dog) have proved to be good companions. Speaking to a pet is better than talking to the walls or mumbling about things when there is no one to hear. The old question "Does a falling tree make a noise when there is no one to hear the sound?" If seniors talk to themselves, they hear a human voice, when there is no one to respond, this further complicates their isolation. The elderly need someone or something to talk to, of course it is better to have a conversation with a person, but meditation and prayer can fill the void when a senior is alone.

Talking to Yourself

Many people, young and old, talk to themselves or speak out loud when they are alone. In some cases it may become a problem, but normally it springs from anxiety or loneliness. Not having someone to talk with creates a human need to speak. Some people talk to themselves when they are organizing their thoughts, others may speak out loud when thinking through a problem to find a solution. It is similar to singing a song when alone to change your mood. It is written in ancient writing that the Prophet Nehemiah "Consulted with himself and got good advice." Do not make talking to yourself or talking out loud when you are alone a problem. This little poem by H. Lynn Green (2014) may assist your thinking.

When you talk to yourself, you have a good listener.
When you whistle a tune, you hear good notes.
When you walk alone, God walks with you.
When you talk out loud, God hears every word.

When you walk alone, God is your companion.
When you talk to yourself, God is always there.
When you whisper a prayer, God always hears.
When you talk to God He hears every word.

When you talk to yourself count it a prayer.
When God hears, He always answers.
Sometimes He says, "yes" - sometimes He says "no"
Sometimes He says "wait a while" - but He answers.

When you talk to yourself, you have a good listener.
When you whistle a tune, you hear good notes.
When you walk alone, God walks with you.
When you talk out loud, God hears every word.

Loved Ones Remain Loved

A tragic aspect of ageing is that seniors often outlive their spouse and many friends. Those we love dearly remain in our hearts even when they are away. This adds to the loneliness of the elderly. When family and friends took a trip, we understood they were just away and would return. Those away remained in our conscious affection and their return was anticipated. As one grows older, family members and dear friends take that long journey into eternity and will not return. Acceptance of the finality of their loss adds to the sense of aloneness. Although they remain loved ones and have a lasting place deep within their sleepless memories, the permanent loss is evident. In fact, the sweet essence of their presence lingers as long as we live, but seniors need fresh compensating relationships to fill this void. Close family members and dear friends can be a Silver Lining in a cloudy memory provided they are present.   Kin or friends that live far away do not fill this emptiness.   Those near must step up and be counted as present. This is the minimum requirement of family.

Remember the Golden Rule is so basic it appears in the sacred writings of most religions:

- **Buddhism** –"Hurt not others in ways that you yourself would find hurtful" (Udana-Vaarga 5,1)

- **Christianity** –"As you would that men should do unto you, do you also to them likewise." (Luke 6:31)

- **Hinduism** – "This is the sum of duty; do naught unto others what you would not have them do unto you." (Mahabharata 5, 1517)

- **Judaism** – "What is hateful to you, do not do to your fellowman. This is the entire Law; all the rest is commentary." (Talmud, Shabbat 3id)

- **Taoism** – "Regard your neighbor's gain as your gain, and your neighbor's loss as your own loss." (Tai Shang Kan Yin P'ien)

Away — but in our Hearts

Those we love clearly remain in our hearts even when they are away. At this point, they remain loved ones, and have a lasting place deep within our conscious memories as long as we live. A Silver Lining in the memory area becomes clear when one understands that loved ones remain loved. This is why people visit a grave site and talk with the deceased. They are not crazy; they remain attached to a loved one. Visiting the grave can facilitate a stronger visual memory. This can enable the elderly to remember people and events based on a photograph or a picture in their mind of an individual or an event. This assists with a positive mental attitude about the past and a sense of purpose about the future.

Find Strength in Serving

Regardless of how strong or weak one may be they find strength when they support others. The joy of volunteering to assist a worthy cause or lend a helping hand to a stranger produces the seeds of real joy. There is no pleasure in life that can equal the joy of assisting the needy or the disadvantaged. When a need is seen, it is pay-back time. Many have expressed the joy of being a volunteer in a soup kitchen, faith-based operation, childcare or eldercare facility, and that the non-material reward greatly outweighs any cash stipend or energy used. In fact, the wealthy who donate large sums to charity receive little tangible benefits, while a poor man sharing his physical energy to assist another in need is reimbursed many times over the value of the deed.

Giving and Sharing

An old fairy tale is told of a goose that laid a golden egg, but the giving of time and energy in physical labor, or a small gift out of poverty brings blessings beyond silver and gold. In fact, the less one has the more valuable the gift of time and energy become. Giving and sharing are great blessings! The ancient record got it right, "It is more blessed to give than to receive." What is the blessedness in sharing?

The giver has something to give, while the receiver is the one with less and sometimes they have less than nothing; that

is, they are poor, sick, and alone. If they are elderly the need
is compounded many times over, because they feel isolated
from home and hearth. To be able to share gifts or energy
is a great blessing. Try it, you will enjoy the ride! As an old
gentleman shared "cast your bread on the water and it will
come back with butter and jam." Also, I am reminded of a little
girl who listened intently to a person sharing about the benefits
of "praying for others." The child responded, "Prayer is just
like jam, you can't spread even a little without getting some on
yourself."

Intrinsic vs. Extrinsic Rewards

There is a theory in motivation that deals with intrinsic
and extrinsic values in the workplace. The conclusion of
several studies was that job satisfaction depended on more
than pay. Individuals who worked for a paycheck were less
satisfied with their labor than those who enjoyed their work and
considered the work meaningful. It appears that the desire to
produce a product or service of value to others brings a level
of satisfaction that money cannot buy.

The intrinsic drive that activated enjoyment in the task
itself actually came from within the person and was not
stimulated by extrinsic or external reward. It appears that the
joy of volunteering and sharing falls in this category; something
within the person that causes them to assist others becomes
a reward in and of itself.   Those who have a "hireling" mindset
and work only for a paycheck are less satisfied with their work
or the product they produce. This validates that there are
genuine blessings in giving or working for the benefit of others.

Enjoy the Benefits

The elderly can assist others and receive lasting benefits
for themselves. Everyone needs assistance in some area
of their life. There was an elderly gentleman named Charlie
Little. He had 12 children. When asked, "Charlie how do you
make it with so many mouths to feed?" Mr. Little's response
was "Every little helps!" Not only does every little help, it
helps the helper more than a little. Find something to do
and do it with all your heart....you will feel better and life will
be a little easier as you move forward.   We can rejoice with

ancient scripture, "Sorrow may endure for the night, but joy comes in the morning." Even a small light will shine brightly in the darkness. It is similar to the first glimmer of light in the morning; it is sunrise of a new day." The new day has 24 hours and 1,440 minutes and many, many moments --make the best of each moment.

Golden Memories

Memories are snap shots of events with personal value and become keepsakes to which we return and reflect from time to time. Good memories are similar to gold in a bank; it is safe and secure and can be used when needed. Those kinds of memories keep our loved ones alive in our hearts. Finally, we will join them in the long sleep. Together at last... together forever! Most of us feel similar to the old gentleman who said, "I didn't want to get old, but since I got old I want to get as old as I can get!" This was a good declaration for a long life.

Bright Side of Clouds

Understanding the ultimate home going and reunion enables most of us to deal with the difficult times of life. Even when the bad days reoccur, the memory of loved ones keeps us focused on the "good ole days" of the past while we consider the future. This is life for us all! The question "Is it life well lived?" As we look on the bright side of the clouds, we see hope and a secure future. Take a short walk with friends and family; it can make a difference in your life today, tomorrow and even next week. To be with friends and see the beauty of nature is a divine blessing.

Life IS A STORY, AND BECOMING
INVOLVED IN THE STORYLINE OF AN
AUTHOR CAN BRING THE ACTION AND
JOY OF LIFE...

6

WALKING

WITH FAMILY AND FRIENDS

Managing Relationship Problems

The loss of patience is an early sign of ageing; especially, with friendships that no longer provide what both parties need and want. When a relationship grows toxic, it may be time to remove them from your "friends list." Remember, friends are similar to money in the bank; one can use the interest without depleting the principle, but when friends are no longer of value they need to be "unfriended." When a friendship no longer benefits both parties it is time to move on. At first, it may be best to discuss how the friendship has changed; then, and only then do you drop a valued friend. Friendship requires lots of transparency and must provide some usefulness for both parties. Perhaps the friendship can be saved, but when it starts to be more painful than pleasurable, it is best to end it. Making new friends is often harder than keeping old ones. Yet one must ask certain questions about each new and existing relationship:

1. Do friends talk about themselves and seem less interested in your situation?

2. Are you left wishing the conversation with friends had been avoided?

3. Does the other party have a personal problem with which they have not or will not adequately deal?

4. Are you miserable around a particular person?

5. Have you deliberately avoided the company of some so called friends?

6. Have these lost other close friends?

7. Do you feel you are wasting time trying to make the friendship work?

Blessings vs. Challenges

Blessings often come disguised as a challenge. This may come as an inspiration to act immediately relative to a recognized need in others. If you wait, you just get older and then the action is harder. If something needs to be done about yourself, your future, or the needs of others, you should do it even if you do not have the money or the time. Some may call it talent or skill, but most of the time achievement comes with the help of a few friends. Real courage comes when you realize you actually need assistance to move forward. This is where true friends become an asset and a blessing. Some say, friends are similar to butter and jam on your bread, but bread may be healthier without butter or jam. After all, friendship is not measured by a bank balance or a retirement fund. To have personal wealth, just count your many friends and look at all the blessings you have that money cannot buy.

Some words of an old song, "Count your Blessings" by Johnson Oatman, Jr. (1897), spoke to this issue:

When upon life's billows you are tempest tossed,
When you are discouraged, thinking all is lost,
Count your many blessings, name them one by one,
And it will surprise you what the Lord hath done.

Are you ever burdened with a load of care?
Does the cross seem heavy you are called to bear?
Count your many blessings, every doubt will fly,
And you will keep singing as the days go by.

So, amid the conflict whether great or small,
Do not be disheartened, God is over all;
Count your many blessings, angels will attend,
Help and comfort give you to your journey's end.

A Small Piece of Paper

The ancient Japanese art of paper folding, Origami, is the ability to make something out of almost nothing. One who has mastered the steps can transform a small square of paper into a bird or other object that brings meditative peace to the person. It is a kind of paper prayer. Origami suggests that individuals can take small, almost insignificant things and create a stress reducing process. Why not try it? It is similar to "cloud watching."

Have you ever watched the clouds and seen it form something: a bird, a plane, a lamb, or a tree? Imagination is the ability to form images and ideas in the mind that brings a sense of resourcefulness to those who would otherwise be idle. Rest is good, but idleness and inactivity is bad. Why is "idleness" bad? Idleness breeds apathy, laziness, redundancy and procrastination. The old adage may be true: "An idle mind is the Devil's workshop." Peace comes through being active, diligent, industrious and otherwise fully engaged in life.

The Devil's Workshop

Most of us were told as children that an "idle mind" was the devil's workshop. If this were true, the converse would also be true: an active mind is a divine workplace. When the body ages and physically slows down, one must keep the mind active. One way is to read a book. Before movies or television, most people handled aloneness by reading stories about faraway places and imaginary people who acted bravely to save a damsel in distress or behaved interestingly in a romantic relationship. While reading the individual is forced to put themselves into the story and experience the emotions, but the modern media has suppressed the imagination by providing almost everything sensory except the smell. This failure to exercise imagination also hinders recall or memory.

Read a Good Book

Many years ago, reading was an enjoyable pastime, but radio, television, computers, the Internet and cell phones have robbed many of the joy of reading. Reading a good book can take you places you cannot go and cause you to see beauty almost beyond your imagination. Reading can lose you in the language, hide you in the action of others, and produce the joy of being there. Good reading is a beneficial pastime for the elderly. If limited eyesight is a problem, petition others to read to you or organize a reading group where you can share in the joy of the narrative. Life is a story and becoming involved in the storyline of an author can bring the action and joy of life to your limited environment. Turn off the TV, hide your cell phone and enjoy the self-control brought about by reading. Television imposes a schedule and scenario on you. The ringing of a phone may bring unsolicited voices, but in reading, the voices and the story are your personal selections. Reading is freedom beyond the mixed-up world in which we all exist. Enjoy the benefits of reading a good book. You may not be able to choose where you live or your present state of health, but you can enjoy the freedom of choice in what you read. To become lost in a well written story or brief unit of action in a dramatic or literary work is one of the great blessings of choice.

Just Thirty Minutes

Reading benefits almost everyone who participates. Just thirty minutes a day can both improve your attitude about personal circumstances of life and your vocabulary for conversation. Reading develops critical thinking and reasoning skills and is a good way to reduce stress. Reading a good book becomes a simple plan for healthy relaxation and distraction from present surroundings; it is a kind of positive escapism from the perceived unpleasant aspects of daily life. Reading becomes wholesome entertainment because one learns about historic figures or gains a perspective on life and living otherwise unavailable. Reading a daily newspaper, a monthly magazine, or a good book allows one to exercise imagination and activates the right side of the brain. This stimulation improves "thinking skills" because the right side controls the more academic and logical side of the brain.

Using the Right Side

The brain is divided into two sides and each part controls specific functions. When one does math, attempts to deal with facts, or studies language, they use the left side of the brain. When one is daydreaming, driving a car, or following a personal intuitive feeling, they use the right side of the brain. This is why reading is important for the elderly; it stimulates the right side of the brain. When one is worrying about money, or where they are going to live, or what they will do tomorrow, the left side of the brain is in control. Reading a good book can switch the control to the right side. Since sacred writings declared "Laughter is like good medicine" then it could also be true: reading a good book is similar to a dose of happiness.

Facilitate Mental Control

Mental control is the issue. Both sides of the brain are connected and switch taking control when necessary. When the right side is in control one normally does not bother themselves with logical patterns and they think in an unconventional way. As one ages, they need to stimulate the right side and permit it to control much of their life. When the right side is in control the person views things in an all-inclusive way, rather than worrying about the details. Since "the devil is in the details" it is good for the elderly to think of the general good rather than the particular bad. This gives individuals a better understanding of real situations. When one exercises the right side of the brain, they have a stronger visual memory and can remember people and events based on a picture they have in their memory. Reading can facilitate this process.

Affordable Lifestyle

Most adults seek an affordable lifestyle as they age. It can be difficult to make good decisions about this process. Anticipating the financial burden of ageing is vital to both health and peace of mind. Can you imagine retirement without the financial worries? Everyone in the family has a stake in the health and safety of the difficult ageing process. When your choice is to remain healthy and happy in your own home or move to assisted-living, let your loved ones assist with your decision. If you remain in your home, you may need assistance with meal preparation, errands, light housekeeping, transportation, laundry, personal hygiene, and companionship.

Everyone needs friends and associates; no one wants to be alone. Humans are at the core social beings. Have a conversation with your family about these issues. Everyone should strive to maintain their personal independence as long as possible. Then when this is no longer possible, make the best of the situation in consultation with family and friends.

A Slippery Slope

It is my firm conviction that when individuals and families show proper concern for their children and parents, the path to a life of quality opens before them. When individuals neglect themselves, their children (or other people's children), their parents or the elderly parents of others, they are on a slippery slope the end of which is misery and disappointment. It is also my firm conviction that a bridge over many of the troubled waters of life could be planned and constructed that will assist adults during stressful times of life and improve both personal and family relationships.   Planning can ease the process of transition for all concerned.

The Pursuit of Happiness

No community effort, program or service is complete that does not take into consideration the needs of children, the elderly and all the adult dynamics that are a part of the process from birth to the last years of life. The primary concern is for the children because they represent the future. At the other end of the journey are the elderly with both their desires and needs. Also, in between the children and the elderly are the lives of many adults who lives are influenced by the way children and the elderly are treated. In every case, the quality of life equation must be balanced to assure that each aspect of life is worth living.

Contentment and Fulfillment

Some call this happiness, while others see contentment and fulfillment coming from the use of faith-based principles and the addition of religious worship. In reality, life is a journey, and the adult pursuit of happiness normally needs a little guidance to focus on the proper objective and good goals of life and career. It is the pursuit of happiness, the actual day-to-day walk that determines the quality of life. Life is not always a bed of roses and all circumstances are not pleasant. Everyone exists within a human culture and humans are not perfect beings. All the people one meets on the journey are not always filled with gladness and helpfulness. However, I believe there is a place, built on faith-based principles, that becomes the foundation for a life of quality and peace. To be surrounded in the final years of life by moral and ethical people in a safe and secure environment, should be the ultimate goal for all the elderly. Most would agree that our parents and grandparents deserve the best we can provide.

Quality of Life Concerns

Here is a baker's dozen of primary concern when considering the quality of life for adults. Why a baker's dozen? Several theories exist about a baker's dozen being 13 instead of 12, but most believe since bread was a primary food source that it was easy for a baker to sell a "light loaf" and cheat patrons. A good baker in turn would put in a 13th loaf to assure proper weight. So I suggest a baker's dozen just to be safe. Maybe that is why the "white" bread in some places is called "light bread" because of weight not color. The list below is a beginning, but there are many more concerns when dealing with the elderly.

1. Attitude toward Social Change
2. Feelings for the Underprivileged
3. Emotional and Social Life
4. Faith-based Connections
5. Financial Affairs
6. Health and Fitness
7. Family Relationships
8. Parenting Skills
9. Personal Nourishment and Diet
10. Social Relationships
11. Spiritual Development
12. Work or a Productive Life
13. A Safe Place to Live and Work

Eldercare Facilities

An elderly care facility ought to provide, not only a safe and secure environment for seniors, but also various opportunities for productive service and sharing with others based on the knowledge and capability possessed by each person. This is one reason Olive's House, was constructed next to the Bridge of Hope childcare facility; it is hopeful that some of the elderly will enjoy becoming surrogate grandparents for the children. At Olive's House the able-bodied elderly will be able to freely associate with and assist in the upbringing of needy children. This will be a double blessing to both the children and the elderly.

Alpha and Omega

The concept of Alpha and Omega ought to be used to guide and evaluate the development of community projects and services. At the Alpha end of life's continuum are the children who must have daily care and a safe place to live and grow within a family-type environment; on the Omega end of the continuum are the elderly who have a right to live and enjoy their golden years in peace, safety, and productivity. The children and the elderly may need assistance to provide for their environment; it is in the adult years, between childhood and the elderly, where individuals are both able and responsible for their own quality of life. We must not neglect either the children or the elderly because to do so will eventually destroy the family and reduce the quality of life for all.

Dealing with Ageing

Dealing with ageing relates directly to the Alpha and Omega, the beginning and the end. My work with children and the elderly, the quality of life effort is to build a bridge across the adult years. These are the most productive and problematic years of life for most people. Ancient sacred writings declared, "Man that is born of woman is of few years and full of trouble." Most of the common sense efforts deal with the difficulties and troubles in the cycle of life.   There is no easy pathway when dealing with adults with difficulties or weakened quality of life because of poor self-image, a bad marriage, financial difficulties, or a wealthy person who uses money as a pacifier and attempts to buy happiness. The truly happy people are those who serve others and put themselves in the background.   Many seniors still have skills and time to volunteer and be useful.   Regardless of where seniors live, home alone, with family, or in an eldercare facility, they need the opportunity to demonstrate their value by using their knowledge and expertise to assist others with something that is positive and productive.

Patient Discharge and Readmission

The hope of most seniors is to remain reasonably healthy and stay in their own home during the final years of life. Also, they wish to avoid even an overnight stay in a medical facility. Preference is to sleep in their own bed in their own home. Yet, most seniors spend many days and nights in a doctor's office or in hospital. With this reality, a secondary objective comes to light: once discharged from a hospital, the wish is not to return. Yet, 1 in 5 seniors who leave a medical facility are readmitted within 30 days. This places strain on the patient, their family, the limits of insurance, and the availability of a healthcare facility space.   The goal of rehab is for the patient to recover sufficient strength to remain at home and avoid readmission.

Transition Care

The patient, their doctors, and the family must collaborate on how to assist a senior's recovery at home and avoid readmission. When a patient is discharged from a medical facility there is normally a transition care plan noted by a physician or a facility to guide the patient and their family to prevent readmission to a medical facility. Many patients are return to a facility for reasons that are preventable because of a failure to review the patient's discharge instructions and insuring the patient is taking all prescribed medicines. Also, there is a need to schedule a follow-up appointment with a physician. The most common diagnoses requiring a return to a medical facility are heart and circulation problems, pneumonia, and breathing difficulties. Proper homecare can lessen the change of returning to full-time medical care, but it takes work on the part of both the patient and the family. For most seniors returning home from a medical facility, there is a need for attention by a home based caregiver, a private nurse, or a day sitting service. Some need ulcer care, treatment for pressure sores, and wound care. The elderly sick must not be left alone for extended periods. Someone must check on them regularly. When this care is provided by a loving family member, there will be a need for relief or downtime for the caregiver and possibly temporary respite care for the patient in a day care or assisted living facility. Some insurance provides for these short-term interval care measures to prevent the readmission to hospital or long-term care.

7

RETAINING
PRODUCTIVITY AND VALUE

Social Media and Hashtags

The various social media use the symbol (#) "hashtag" for many aspects of life and communication. Often it deals with negative comments about "something" going on in society. The elderly must see (#) hashtag as an opportunity to express themselves in many aspects of life. It is in this light that the elderly, in an effort to keep up with the times and remain relative, must continue to remain productive and retain their self-worth and the values they developed over a life time. Seniors must feel free to express themselves to anyone who will listen. The wisdom of the elderly is needed in this troubled world.

Planting the Seeds of Hope

All faith-based people must emphasize the necessity of peaceful meditation, prayers and thanksgiving to be adequately prepared to influence positive change in the lives of others. A religious leader once asked an elderly member how she felt. Her answer, "My condition is pretty good considering my condition." She was pressed for more information. Her response, "Well, friend, I feel better now than I did a while ago." The visitor was still unaware of her "condition," but she expressed herself. After all that was the reason for the question: to give her an opportunity to express her feelings, not to inform the visitor of her medical condition. Sharing a feeling is planting the seed of hope. Once the words are forthcoming, the patient usually feels better.

Always Positive

There is an old story of a mother who tried to always be positive. She tried to never say "no" to her children. Her young daughter asked, "Mother, may I go outside and play?" Her response was "Yes, when your brother gets home from school." Another question from the son, "Mother may I have an ice cream?" The answer was, "Yes, when we go to the store on Friday." This mother went through life with a positive attitude. The children grew up and married, the daughter visited and made lunch for her mother and asked, "Mother, I made some tea, do you have any ice cubes?" "Yes, but they are not frozen yet" was the positive answer. Would it not be great if we could always be positive? Upbeat, optimistic, constructive, and encouraging expressions are a confident way to live and feel secure. These are the marks of maturity. Positive expressions often provide a hopeful future and eliminate some of the negativity that fills many lives. The absence of a positive attitude brings doubt into daily life and breeds negative behavior. There is no place in family life for negativity that fosters refusal and denial. Ancient sacred writings recorded a useful adage "A soft answer turns away wrath."

Life Experience Produces Expertise

A lifespan of 60 plus years develops experience and readily bestows expertise on seniors. This capability and know-how provides the resources, authority, and the opportunity for each person to age gracefully and live a life larger than otherwise expected. There is a story of a gracious elderly lady, when mailing an old family Bible to her younger brother for safe keeping, the postal clerk asked, "Is there anything breakable in here?" The firm and clear answer was "Only the words of the Prophets and a few Commandments." We must never break the chain of wisdom that reaches back to the sages of old, the teaching of parents, and to the pages of sacred writings. Life experience creates an expertise that opens many doors for the elderly to remain creative and useful into their later years. All who fail to avail themselves of the opportunity to acquire the expertise of seniors will miss good and exchangeable units of wisdom and an exceptional knowledge base built upon years of community and public service. Using the expertise of the elderly is to find solutions for many current difficulties and prevent some future problems. This can be done by using solutions already found to everyday problems that seem to recur in each generation.

Positive and Respectful Contacts

The contacts and interaction between adults, the elderly and the next generation must be both positive and respectful. There must be an orderliness of operation and practical arrangements for all generational conversation. The efficiency of all adult services and the effectiveness of senior programs must be evaluated and weaknesses strengthened and the benefits utilized to the advantage of all concerned. When adults neglect the needs of children or their elderly parents, the long-term existence of family values are weakened or abandoned. To neglect either the children or the elderly is disgraceful, immoral, and shameful.

A Family Decision

It can be difficult to make wise decisions about final stage housing. Everyone in the family has a part in the emotional health of all members. If the choice is to remain healthy and happy in your home, or move in with family, or make the move to assisted care, let your family assist with the decision. If you remain in your home, you may need assistance with meal preparation, errands, light house-keeping, transportation, laundry, companionship, and personal hygiene. Have a conversation with the extended family about all these matters. Maintain personal independence as long as possible. Anticipating the financial burden on the family and the limited assets of the senior is vital to both health and happiness. Can you imagine retirement without financial worries? Life must be something more than long. Quality counts. Being healthy and active are two of life's greatest pleasures. Don't tiptoe forward, embrace the ageing process. This is the best way to remain both healthy and happy.

Changing Times

Old age is not a rare disease from which the rest of humanity is immune. For those fortunate enough to have a long life, the problems of ageing will be forthcoming with the same vengeful sorrows presently being experienced by seniors. Notwithstanding the increase in medical science and compassionate governments, the present neglect of needy seniors could produce the worse stain on humanity in decades. There was a time when older adults lived out their relatively peaceful lives in their own homes or with their children. Times have changed. The elderly who cannot care for themselves are often neglected while their children enjoy the fruits of parental labors. Remember, what goes around, comes around. What will you do when it becomes your turn to suffer the ravages of neglect by family and friends? Misfortune may come to some, but hopefully it will not be retribution for the past neglect of parents. This must not happen in a civilized society.

Neglect of Parents is a Mockery

A reprehensible practice of adult children avoiding responsibility for the needs of parents was clearly observed in Old Testament times. Neglect in the name of religion is a mockery of both family and God. The Talmud recorded that some Jews would make false vows at the Temple concerning funds for their parents without intention of keeping the vow. Adults would tell their parents that all funds were dedicated to a sacred purpose and that none were available for their support. This absurdity was utilized as if caring for one's parents was not a sacred task. Attention to this travesty showed the disregard of a clear commandment of God: the one requiring children to honor and respect their father and mother. The term "respect" meaning, *to look at and pay attention to*. In the case of the elderly, "honor" may include the expenditure of funds in the care of ageing parents.

Policy and Practice

A philosophy of life in relation to the elderly must include a positive attitude that values and informs both policy and practice in response to the events and quality of life for senior citizens. This cannot be left to government agencies alone, there must be personal and community involvement to assure compassion and to put a human face on the process. Governmental involvement may be needed, but it is second-best to personal and private expressed concern for the elderly. With a positive community concern, the elderly would have a positive perspective on life with healthy consequences including attitude and behavior that informs a future with optimism and security. These together with opportunities and plans for happy years ahead would give the clouds of the ageing years a Silver Lining.

General Well-being

The term "quality of life" is used to evaluate the general well-being of individuals. The concept is used widely in different contexts: in this case, it deals only with an intervention in the lives of individuals with general dissatisfaction with their personal or professional life. Quality of life should not be confused with the concept of the standard of living, which is based primarily on income. While quality of life has long been both an explicit or implicit goal for my work, an adequate definition and assessed value has been elusive. There are both objective and subjective indicators across a range of disciplines and scales, and recent work on the subjective well-being surveys and the psychology and philosophy of happiness have spurred renewed interest. Included in related concepts to quality is the use of faith-based principles to guide both life and living. When life is related to faith in a Higher Power as a Guide, a better quality of life is the normal outcome. General happiness is a byproduct of faith-based quality of life.

Related Concepts

Also related are concepts such as personal freedom, individual rights, and happiness that have intruded on marriage and family as well as the professional and business areas. Since so many of the indicators are subjective and cannot be directly measured; it becomes necessary to develop an instrument to surrogate these qualities and assess them indirectly. For example, "How much does a man love his wife?" This cannot be directly measured but must be indirectly assessed through a developed index. What is obvious is that increased income or actual wealth does not directly impact the quality of life. Consequently, standard of living will not be taken as criteria for quality of life. Yet, several assessed areas will be considered as having some influence on the quality of life. It is my clear conviction that faith-based principles and the qualities of spiritual development can greatly influence the quality of life for adults. An adequate spiritual foundation can assist an individual or a couple over the troubled waters of life and bring a renewed quality and quantity to life. A survey instrument will be developed to assess the area of risk management that impact quality of life for individuals in their later years.

Quality of Life Survey

A Quality of Life survey instrument should be used by eldercare facilities as a screening tool for individuals who desire significant change in various areas of their life. Results may highlight areas that require change to improve their quality of life. The survey instrument gathers data on the relationship between an individual's quality of life and other behaviors. This will be an assessment using indirect measurements to develop a basis for guidance and mentoring elderly individuals and senior couples. Major areas for consideration are:

- Aesthetic Satisfaction
- Benevolent Behavior
- Career/work Satisfaction
- Communications Behavior
- Emotional Maturity
- Extended Family Relations
- Faith-based Concerns
- Financial Security
- Future Concerns
- Happiness Measure
- Health/Fitness Measure
- Inter-personal Relations

- Leisure/Vacation Behavior
- Marital Relations
- Parenting Relations
- Personal Growth
- Physical Fitness Indicators
- Security Concerns
- Self-Image Concerns
- Social Activity
- Daily Stress Level
- Sense of Well-Being

The Gratitude Meter

The best way forward is to remember, with gratitude the good things of the past. Remembering the best days of the past can produce a feeling of joy and gratitude and cause one to "share" or pay forward the feeling of genuine gratitude. Being grateful for the past pleasures of life can produce a thankfulness that demonstrates itself in appreciation for the action and words of others. Pay forward the joy by expressing gratitude for what others do and who others are. Acknowledge their smile, their friendliness, their neat clothing or well-groomed appearance. Expressing acknowledgment of a benefit received from others will produce a predisposition to act positively around others. Learn to unleash an abundance of happiness to others through the power of gratitude. This attitude is catching. Friendliness cannot be taught; it is caught by observation. Ancient writings expressed, "To have friends, one must show a friendly attitude." Check the dial on your gratitude meter regularly and keep it on the positive side. At the senior stage of life one should focus on making others happy. It will return in many ways. As one man said, "Cast your bread on the water and it will return with butter and jam."

Meaningful Memories

Do you remember growing up? Can you recall a pleasant family tradition? Meaningful memories of the past can bring a ray of sunshine to your day. It can also brighten the day for those around you. A smile is contagious. Friendliness grows and expands. Sharing good memories brings good thoughts to those about you. Share personal enthusiasm. Emphasize the positive, eliminate the negative, and leave all negativity in the dark place where you found it or throw it into the sunlight where it will dissolve into nothingness. Enthusiasm originally meant inspiration provided by a divine presence. Individuals can be a source of inspiration by sharing the good memories with others. This will bring real meaning to your life and increase your confidence in the future.

A Sense of Gratitude

Life is filled with daily problems that need to be solved, and recurring difficulties which create stress. Research is continually finding that expressing thanks can lead to a healthier, happier life. In expressing herself on this issue many years ago, Martha Washington said, "The greater part of our misery and unhappiness is determined not by our circumstance, but by our disposition." Ralph Waldo Emerson once said that in order to achieve contentment, one should "cultivate the habit of being grateful for every good thing that comes to you, and to **give thanks continuously**." Not only do you outlive your enemies, but at times there is joy in realizing that you have outlived some of your friends!

A Gratitude Journal

Keeping a gratitude journal for some seems to provide a wellness benefit. Writing down things for which one is thankful enables the brain to focus more clearly on positive issues. It is obvious that in most cases, people focus on what goes wrong rather than the positive aspects of life. Keeping a journal can assist one in moving forward toward personal goals. Dealing with good things enables one to deal with the other side of the coin. In most lives, the good outweighs the bad, provided an effort is made to remember and appreciate the good things. Remembering a bad experience from the past or a hard time can cause one to feel grateful for their present state of affairs. Look around, your life is better than many other seniors. Be grateful for what you have!

Pay Forward Kindness

Thankful people seem to more easily pay forward the kindness they experience. It has been suggested that as one grows older they should initiate a kind of "**Operation: C.A.K.E.**" and do some **C**haritable **A**cts of **K**indness **E**veryday. Most everyone loves cake, so why not pass it on in the form of human kindness shared with those around you. According to research published by the University of North Carolina, the little things and daily gratitude interactions increased relationship connection and overall satisfaction for both men and women. One of the little things is to "volunteer" to assist others, even doing little jobs. It appears that such action can result in less depression and increased overall well-being. It has been suggested that the elderly should examine their personal talents and expertise and volunteer to help others, noting that people become more grateful as givers rather than receivers. Ancient sacred writings recorded that "it is more blessed to give than to receive." Just as giving a gift can clear the mind and reduce personal stress, people who become more charitable seem to experience a healthier lifestyle. Consequently, sharing what you have with others and volunteering to assist where you can becomes one of the best medicines.

Fellowship is Friendship

Fellowship among the elderly is not a costume party where one drags out old tattered garments of the past and parades it before the group. True fellowship is real friendship, where folks are in the same boat on a sunlit lake enjoying the afternoon. It is not a hostile ship filled with noise and confusion. In other words, friend-ship is not a battleship lobbing missiles at others; it is a rowboat in smooth water moving toward the sunlight. Friendship is effortless and smooth where one does not sweat the small stuff. Friends can help one cope when moving to affordable housing. In fact, good friends are better than money in the bank. Why? You can use the interest without depleting the principal.

This IS A NEW DAY, YOU MUST
BECOME A NEW YOU.

8

MOVING
TO AFFORDABLE HOUSING

Influencing the Happiness of the Elderly

Building healthy and happy communities for active seniors includes more walking space, green areas, trails, flower gardens, and parks. Enlarged signage is welcomed as well as a wheelchair accessible trail system, and a fitness center suitable for all abilities. The elderly gradually begin to lose functioning ability or have other health issues, and usually require assistance as they grow older. The secret to happiness for most seniors is for them to live in a home-style situation that simulates their own living quarters. Using personal pieces of furniture and family pictures are important to their sense of well-being.

Possible Areas of Conflict

There are common ethical or legal issues that confront eldercare providers. Legal precedent is established that parents have an obligation to financially support their children. In turn, it has been an acceptable practice for eldercare to be provided within the extended family with the expense accepted by family members. Since governments, NGO's, nonprofits, and private business have entered the eldercare arena, facilities that provide services for the elderly must follow currently stated guidelines and regulations provided by governments or a third party. Allowing seniors to live out the

final years of life in one place with flexible accommodation
that are designed to meet their health and housing needs
are covered in such guidelines. There are several situations
under which conflict may arise when family members and
professional caregivers assist or represent the elderly. They
include:

- Conflicts involving children and their wishes versus the
  senior's wishes and interests;

- Conflicts involving extended family members and their
  wishes versus the senior's interest;

- Conflicts involving ethical or legal issues (such as a
  guardian, conservator or agent under a power of attorney)
  who may have interests different than the senior; and

- Conflicts involving the business interest of the facility owner
  or the eldercare providers versus the senior's interests, well-
  being and quality of life.

Senior Places for Living

There are many places for retirement: condos on the
beach, floating ships at sea, retirement communities, assisted
living facilities, eldercare homes, and places to receive
medical care and places to receive final care. However, many
of the elderly cannot afford such places. Many others prefer to
remain in the home with family or near relatives and friends.

Housing for the Poor

There is little housing prepared for the post-poverty/
pre-middle class poor. This elderly group in the middle of
the low-to-moderate-income group, has no name and has
never been specifically classified by any government, but is
composed of hard working seniors, who paid taxes, raised
a family, and now have little or no income and live with the
limitations of a government stipend and/or company pensions.
My friends and I have initiated a remedy for this problem. The
initial project was OLIVE'S HOUSE in Trinidad, a project that
provides low-cost retirement housing in a campus setting,
built adjoining Bridge of Hope, a childcare facility. The vision
of Olive's House was to create a retirement community that
redefined the philosophy of life for the elderly citizens so they
feel connected, respected, and encouraged to live a full life

with meaningful involvement and a hopeful attitude about the future.

Home vs. A Strange Place

The thought of moving from the familiarity of their home and switching to a strange place creates an unhappy person. Although one cannot generalize from the results about the happiness of all the elderly, past studies found that formal education, gender, and geographical areas can influence happiness. As the population ages the need for senior friendly accommodations becomes increasingly important. The goal for all eldercare facilities should be to build an affordable and healthy community to insure a pleasant and agreeable living experience. Facilities are designed to cut down on commutes and environmental harm; preserve open space; encourage community collaboration; and mix land uses with full access for family and friends.

Rehabilitation is the Ticket Home

Upon discharge from a medical facility, staff or a case manager will normally recommend a rehab facility that can assist the patient toward their maximum recovery and return to home. Yet, before you accept the recommended short-term care, know your options and plan ahead. Word of mouth works; family and friends who have had physical therapy can recommend a place that provides physical care and comfort at a price your insurance or family budget can afford. Always take note of limited insurance coverage and available family funds. So, before you check-out of a hospital, know what the next step is in your recovery. The goal is to turn your wellness and health goals into achievements based on affordability.

Rehabilitation facilities are designed to enable the patient to go home again. Every senior deserves to be healthy, happy and a home to enjoy family and friends during the last phase of their journey. For this reason, rehabilitation is important. No one expects to be sick or injured; it is the furthest thing from one's mind. However, when one falls, or is struck down by a stroke or for any reason finds themselves in a medical facility, their greatest hope is to go home again. This is what rehabilitation services are all about. The services of a rehab facility are designed to get you back to functioning at a level where you can live at home, enjoy your family, and hopefully feel productive. Without rehab, most patients will not reach their full potential.

Problems with Living Alone

This book is not about dying; it is about living the final decade in relative contentment in a secure environment near family and friends. There will come a time when most seniors will need some assistance. What are the options? **Residential Facility Housing** for able-bodied seniors and the ambulatory elderly. **Respite Care** is short-term care in the home for a few days and serves individuals unable to care for themselves when family members or those persons normally providing the care need a rest. **24-hour Care** makes available 24/7 treatment in a home environment with multiple or single caregivers depending on the need of the patient. **Assisted Living Facilities** for those who cannot live alone and need personal care, homemaker services and medication assistance for an extended period. **Skilled Senior Care Facility** for those who need daily observation and a medical watch. **Hospice Care** is designed for comprehensive care to patients and families facing the end of life difficulties. Hospice emphasizes pain relief and calming care rather than curative treatments that may increase life for a few days. Comfort and sophisticated symptom relief are provided by professionals.

Happiness for Seniors Includes:

- Keeping in touch with family and friends
- Feeling safe and secure
- Having adequate medical care
- Enjoying a balanced diet
- Having adequate physical therapy and exercise
- Remaining useful and productive
- Reunions with children and grandchildren
- Receiving cards and letters from family and friends
- Enjoying a Birthday Cake and Presents
- Interacting with children and young people

- Faithfully maintaining their personal religion
- Sharing with others their life experience

A Move to Affordable Housing

Olive's House is part of Project **H. O. P. E.** --**H**ousing **O**pportunities **P**repared for **E**lderly and was planned in four stages: 1. Residential Facility Housing for able-bodied couples and the ambulatory elderly; 2. Assisted Living Facilities for those who cannot live alone; 3. Skilled Senior Care Facility for seniors who need daily observation and a medical watch; and 4. A Hospice-type facility for the terminally ill.

Take Responsibility

If age and present health require you and your family to seek an eldercare facility for assistance, be certain the facility is the right fit for all concerned: a place planned with special age-related design and appropriate staff and programs. Survey the situation and make the best use of each opportunity and take responsibility for this phase of your life.

Continuing Eldercare Facility

If you or your spouse are relatively healthy now, but anticipate significant health problems down the line, you may want to consider a Continuing Eldercare Facility. Olive's House is an Eldercare facility located in Trinidad, a Caribbean isle of tropic beauty, offers a range of care from independent living to a daily medical watch in the same community. If residents begin to need assistance with the activities of daily living, they can transfer from independent living to an assisted living unit or a nursing unit on the same site. The main benefit of such a continuing care facility is that patient only needs to relocate once to a new environment and can maintain their independence for a longer period.

New Neighbors and New Environment

Moving to an independent living facility may be stressful. In addition to adjusting to independent living in a new environment, you will be meeting new neighbors and be introduced to a new routine. This may cause some anxiety, but there are things you can do to make the transition to independent living easier:

- Do your homework on the independent living facility and make sure all of your questions are answered ahead of time. It will be less stressful if you know what to expect.

- Make sure you have space for your most important possessions—a favorite armchair or treasured bookcase, and some family photographs, for example.

- Do not add to the stress of the actual move by putting yourself in a position where you will need to make hasty decisions about what to take and what to discard. Pack well in advance of your moving date.

- When you arrive, you may be tempted to stay in your apartment or room, but you will feel comfortable much quicker if you get out and meet the other residents, participate in activities, and explore the conveniences and comforts of the facility. You may actually have old friends there!

- Individuals adjust differently to change; if it is taking longer than you felt it should to adjust, talk to a family member, a trusted friend or a counselor at the facility. Go easy on yourself.

New Day — New You!

This is a new day, you must become a new you. Do not let the past, present circumstance, or age difficulties become hurdles you can't get over. It may be easier than you think to move ahead with your life, provided you take advantage of the opportunities. Your health may not be perfect, but you have made it this far and you still have stamina and grit. With a strong will nothing can hold you back unless you fail to get enough sleep, eat a proper diet, exercise daily, take you medications, and seek to accomplish something worthwhile each day. With the proper attitude and positive action, you can make the rest of your life the best of your days.

Let the Good Times Roll

The baggage carried by the elderly is less important than the person or the forward journey. Most of the events of the past are heavy loads for ageing seniors to carry into the present. Sure, there are some good memories, but the negative aspects of the past often crowd out the positive. The elderly should not dwell on the past; it will hinder their forward progress. Regrets and discouragements are heavy burdens that slow the journey and bring sadness to the remaining days. The past cannot be changed, only the present is important. Let the good times roll!

A Pilot Project

Olive's House was a pilot project that proposed to build senior home units, on a site in proximity to the Bridge of Hope childcare facility, as a model for senior living. The able-bodied seniors could live in the property as their home as long as they were ambulatory. Then additional facilities would be available as their needs reached progressive stages: Assisted Living; Skilled Senior Care; and a Hospice-type facility for the terminally ill.   Each stage would provide adequate caregivers to ensure a secure and healthful environment all on one campus.

A Two-way Opportunity

The proximity of Olive's House to needy children at the Bridge of Home childcare facility provides a two-way opportunity: children who have been deprived of parents and grandparents will have access to surrogate grandparents. Also, the elderly often separated from their own grandchildren will have opportunities to open their hearts and talents to assist with filling the void in the life of a disadvantaged child and in turn will receive the affection and enjoy the laughter of a child. The need is extensive and growing.   We must provide a hopeful future for both the elderly and the children. Living in a place similar to Olive's House should be part of the plan.

L. I. F. E. in Olive's House could mean:

Living a good and healthy life;
In a safe community environment;
Filled with friends and the sounds of laughter; and
Enjoy a campus designed with age-appropriate activities.

A Hopeful Future

With the construction of Olive's House as a complex for Eldercare, senior citizens have an opportunity for a hopeful future.   This is the quality of life our parents deserve and the respectful honor due those who sacrificed to grow their families and build a moral country.   Hopefully, others will initiate similar projects in their community. There was a growing need for a facility designed to assist these seniors with the basic care they require.

Basic care:

To enhance the dignity, independence, and quality of life.

To foster interaction among seniors and the community.

To recruit and promote the services of volunteers.

To maintain a sense of usefulness and add value to their lives.

Services include:

A fully operational Welcome Center

Fully furnished, double occupancy living units

Multi-purpose lounge and entertainment area

Therapeutic Massages

Age-appropriate Gym

Hair and Beauy Salon

Games and Recreation Area

Landscaped gardens and leisure areas

STAGE ONE

Residential Facility
—for couples and ambulatory elderly.

Olive's House as a part of PROJECT: HOPE, seeks to provide housing for the post-poverty/pre-middle class poor. This elderly group in the middle of the low-to-moderate-income group, not specifically classified by the government, but is composed of hard working persons, who paid taxes, raised a family, and now their pensions are not sufficient to provide affordable, safe and age-specific housing for their declining years. The average elderly person living on pension does not have a home and is often forced to live with family or children. These persons cannot afford a condo, a retirement village, or rent for a decent housing opportunity.

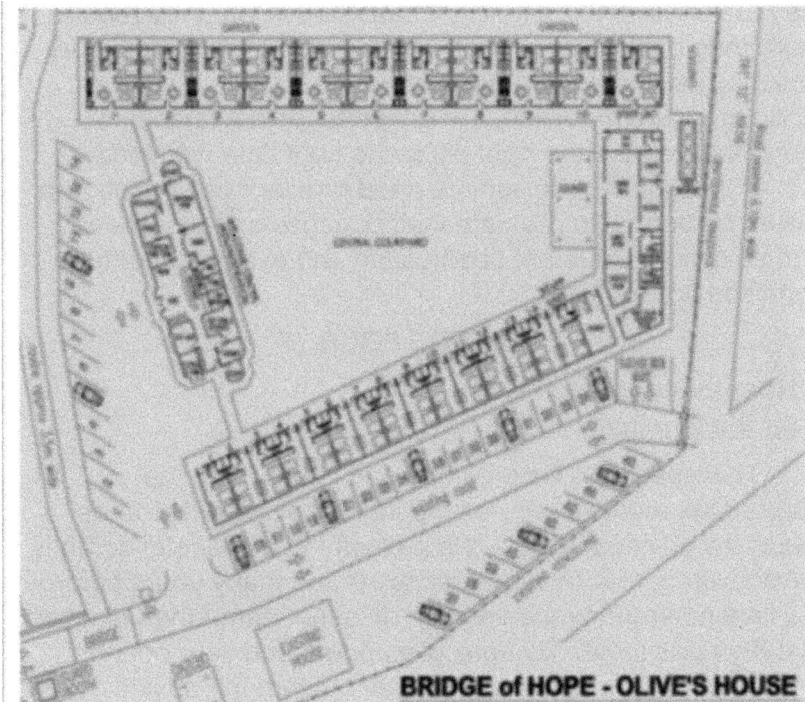

BRIDGE of HOPE - OLIVE'S HOUSE

Site Plan for Olive's House Campus

STAGE TWO

Assisted Living Facilities

—for those who cannot live alone.

The elderly are prone to accidents and at times cannot live alone. Others are unable to do basic housekeeping, cook, shop for groceries and need a helping hand. Most cannot afford a live-in companion or a regular nurse so they must move to assisted living or become a burden to their family. Often their mate has passed and the children live away or have migrated.

STAGE THREE

Skilled Senior Care Facility

—for seniors who need daily medical watch.

When the quality of life of a senior deteriorates to the point they are beyond the capacity of assisted living, they require more than basic services. They may not be fully ambulatory and may be unable to regulate their medications; such as, blood pressure medicine, insulin shots, or just unable to remember to take the right pill at the right time with food, etc. At this point these seniors need regular observation and skilled personnel to regulate their dosages and timeliness of medication. Constant observation and evaluation of their condition are required.

STAGE FOUR

A Hospice-type Facility
—for the terminally ill.

This space will be provided and staffed with the appropriate medical care as the individual need becomes medically obvious. Sadly, the pathway to a peaceful death is paved with decisions about money made many years before the final emergency experience. It is the fear of the unknown that frightens most. Be sure you understand your options. Speak to family members you trust. Accept the advice of loyal friends. Listen to the counsel of a spiritual leader. Follow your doctor's instructions. You will find that there are special people who are prepared to hold your hand and speak words of comfort during the final phase of life. One thing is certain: death can be a friend. Release from suffering and painful struggle. Death is the ultimate healing of the body. In the afterlife, you will have a new and healthy body. This is a divine promise to those who believe and live according to sacred writings.

The Long Goodbye

Finding a smooth path forward is important to all concerned. Understanding the painful certainty of the long goodbye is crucial to the clarity and charity required as one approaches the end of life issues. With the aches and pains of ageing and perhaps the absence of family and friends, a desperate need is created for acceptance of physical limitations, human illness, and existing living arrangements. This is not punitive or vindictive for some past "failures;" it is a normal part of living. Death is the final deliverance; the final

healing of all ailments. Death solves all problems. Death
is an open door to an Afterlife in the Hands of a Loving God.
A magnificent and calming truth, "Earth has no sorrow that
eternity cannot heal." One elderly gentleman describing his
final days, shared with a friend, "I am doing well under the
circumstances." Acceptance of "under the circumstances"
in the final stages of life is the first step in being able to
overcome the consequences of any feelings of desperation
or misfortune. An inscription found painted on a rock informs
such a situation:

> *"Lord, help me to remember that nothing*
> *Will happen to me today that you and*
> *I together can't handle."*

Facing the Final Days

Most of us do not know how to combat the common
enemy called "death," that creeps upon us all. The tragedy
is that each person must face this adversary alone equipped
only with the moral teachings from their religion. Personal
behavior during the final days of life reveals not only character,
but it provides evidence of a life well lived. Recently, a man
was diagnosed with terminal cancer. He accepted the finality
of the physician's statement and demonstrated the courage
of his life-long convictions. He would take the positive path
forward without fear or regret. His primary concern was not
for himself, but for his family and friends. He began to call
them one by one and share the news of his numbered days. A
family reunion was planned so he could see everyone face-
to-face and share memories of the good times. He spoke to
all his close friends and never expressed regret for his life or
any negativity about his future. He was cared for at home
as long as the family was physically and emotionally able to
provide for his needs. Then he was moved to a hospice unit
for terminal patients and because of his positive attitude lived
many months and seemed to enjoy each and every day of
life. Each time friend or family visited him he would share a
memory of a positive event that had brought joy to his life. In
the conversation, he always shared, "This is a nice place.
They really do take good care of you. Anything I want I just

push this little button and they bring it to me. This is a good place."

In God's Hand

During his final days, he chatted on the phone with family and friends and was always positive. His only sister, a cousin who was a retired minister and his mother were his final visitors. At his grave site, the final words were based on Isaiah 49: 15, 16 they recalled that God's love was even stronger than a mother's love; that God had engraved him in the palm of His Hand, and that God knew where he lived and always remembered the circumstances of his life. In fact, I have a small carved statue from Liberia, West Africa of a person in the palm of a hand and carved on the bottom is Isaiah 49:15, 16. This is a message we must all remember, God always remembers us and we are all in the Hands of God. And a loving God knows our "walls" and exactly where we live and He understands our limitations. This is a great comfort to all who accept the affection of divine guidance and care.

Few Get their Wish

Who will write the final chapter of our lives? In today's world, most of the elderly want to die peacefully at home surrounded by family and friends. One gentleman shared, "I want to die in my sleep of something I didn't know I had." Few get such a wish. However, seniors may execute a document called a living will or an advanced directive and control the final days of life. Such legal documents spell out the types of medical treatments and life-sustaining measures desired and those refused. Living wills may be called healthcare declarations or healthcare directives. Medical or healthcare power of attorney (POA) is a document that designates an individual, referred to as a healthcare agent/proxy, to make medical decisions in the event a patient is unable to act. This is different from a POA authorizing someone to make financial transactions. Family and doctors should be consulted if questions or disagreements arise. Before a move is made to an Eldercare Facility A Checklist for Application for Residency ought to be reviewed and completed. (**See Appendix Four**)

Preparation for Ageing and Death

The ultimate problem is the process of dying. Everyone will die and many do not fear death, but see death as the final healing and the ultimate gift of life without problems or pain. Those who do not fear death often express anguish about the process of dying. Something must take everyone out the physical world and into the next life, but just what that will be and the exact process is unknown. Will death come by a natural disaster, human accident, extended famine, unjust war, debilitating disease, or just the creeping years of the ageing process until the body just wears out?

Hospice is Not a Bad Word

Death with dignity is the hope of most, but few will experience a "peaceful" death without medical intervention. The method that emphasizes pain relief and calming care is a move in the right direction, but the very word "hospice" frightens most because it speaks of terminal illness and end of life issues. "Palliation" means to relieve or lessen without curing - even when the issues are disguised with the words "palliative care" in an effort to mitigate or conceal the gravity of the situation, "hospice" remains a word a patient or the family does not want to hear because it provides no hope for recovery.

Hospice care brings compassion, dignity and hope to patients nearing the end of life. Normally, this is care the family alone cannot provide. For many seniors living with life-limiting illness, there comes a time when a cure is no longer possible, but that does not mean the patient and family must abandon all hope. Through hospice care, there is hope for a peaceful death, time to spend final months, weeks, or days free of pain, and hope for quality time with loved ones. A common sentiment of families who have been assisted by hospice care is that they wish they had known about hospice care sooner.

At this point in the process, the only secure hope resides in personal faith in an "afterlife." Most adults have accepted the concept of life after death as a self-evident anchor that stabilizes them in times of personal anguish.

An Anchor of the Soul

The Hebrews, the Ancient Egyptians, the Indian religions and early Christians believed in an afterlife, also known as life after death and eternal life. Common in such belief systems, an individual's identity or consciousness continued after the death of the body. Belief in an afterlife may be naturalistic or supernatural, but it is in contrast to the concept of oblivion after death. Most religions and many individuals believe that life itself is preparation for an extended existence. However, various religions have different versions of what this afterlife would be. Those who accept the system of reincarnation have a specific view that they will exist in the future based on direct and personal behavior, but are not assured of what life-form that existence will be. On the other hand, those of the Christian faith developed the concept of "a new creation" where the present life is drastically altered by divine intervention in preparation for the afterlife. In this consequence, believers have assurance of a spiritual existence after the death of the body. It is at the point of death that these belief systems bring assurance to the process of dying. The faith that brings hope of continued existence becomes an anchor of the soul.

A Smooth Path Forward

While visiting a dying friend, he said, "I have fixed everything I know to fix, but if you ever run across someone I have offended I authorize you to ask their forgiveness for me." He was finishing all his unfinished business. Now he was on a smooth path forward to a new and better life.

9

FINDING

A SMOOTH PATH FORWARD

The Backstory

The past is an introduction to all that comes after. This is another way to say "history repeats itself." One should never forget that the first part of life prepares you for the rest of your life. The early stages of life are what made you what you are today. The former history of an individual is predictive of what will happen in the future. Why? The backstory prepares us for an increased appreciation for the present. If your past was unproductive or uneventful, the future will most likely be the same. If you lived an exciting life, your future should also be exciting and enjoyable. However, if you consider your backstory to be unproductive, then you will probably be disappointed with the last miles of the journey unless you are able to reframe your mind-set and move toward a positive attitude about living. The backstory may not be changed, but the present can still be upbeat and constructive. File the backstory in the bottom drawer and write an update that things have changed for the better.

The Mindset

A person with a lackadaisical, halfhearted, easygoing attitude throughout life may face their senior years with the same mindset. They most likely would suffer from fatigue, dullness, and a hands-off approach to others, unless they change their attitude by changing their activities. Otherwise, they would be dull and lethargic with others. This would be a dark cloud over their later years without a Silver Lining. On the other hand, a person who was punctual, positive, humorous, and friendly in the past would continue to be gentle, calm, temperate, restful, and friendly with others. The cloudy days of ageing could have a Silver Lining. This lifestyle is possible for most seniors who develop a positive mindset.

Maintaining a Hopeful Future

Early one morning a tremendous cracking sound suddenly awakened a young climber and his guide camping high in the mountains. The young man thought it was the end of the world. The experienced guide explained that it was just the dawning of a new day. As the sun rose and thawed the ice, the melting caused both movement and noise. The climber was told not to view the mountain from the previous sunset, but to see it clearly at the sunrise. Many elderly fall into this trap and fail to see the sunrise as the start of a new day, week, month, year, or decade. Some view their present circumstance as sunsets rather than the dawning of a new, bright opportunity. Tomorrow is the first day of the rest of your life.

Later Stages of Life

As people approach the later stages of life, they often look back to past failures or dwell on present disappointments and permit these facts to define their future. One never reaches a positive conclusion beginning with a negative outlook. A negative mind will pull down the whole body. In a different context, but with the same intent, ancient writings declared "if the smallest toe hurts, the whole body feels the pain." Consequently, when one brings negative thoughts into the mind, the whole body can suffer. We must all make the best of the circumstances in which we find ourselves and accept the challenges of life as opportunities to demonstrate our maturity and ingenuity. Throughout history it was the creative initiative of a few that solved problems and overcame the difficulty that brought about the great inventions. Without the cleverness and resourcefulness of those who saw the problems and went about solving them, we would all be walking barefoot, living in caves, sleeping on the ground, and eating whatever we could find along the pathways or scavenge in the forest. To be alive in the twenty-first century is to enjoy the benefits of the past problem solvers. The best solution to any negative situation is to find a positive path forward.

Second Wind

Life is a marathon, a lengthy, long-drawn-out adventure through good times and bad times. Athletes, hikers, runners, mountain climbers, and all who do labor intensive work soon learn they have two sets of muscles in their legs: walking muscles and running muscles. The physical reality is that when the walking muscles get tired, one must use the running muscles. Then, as one runs the walking muscles rest and are ready for use when the running muscles fatigue. This provides a kind of "second wind" endurance for the long haul, but an awareness of this strength must be developed.

Strength and Endurance

When a young man enlists for military service, he begins a rough training course to build strength and endurance. Why? They know that hardships and struggles will come in the future and they will need the stamina previously developed in training. Why do these people perform important duties and achieve great things? They had developed a winning attitude, a team spirit, a family relationship, a work ethic, and a desire to achieve. They were aware that others were dependent on their efforts and that failure would bring disappointment and discouragement to others. This winning attitude and group awareness made them realize they were a vital part of a whole and gave them self-worth and improved their self-image. It is this spirit of community that is a Silver Lining in the ageing process. When the going gets tough, some use their stamina and "second wind" to push ahead.

Problem using the "second wind"

The central problem with utilizing the "second wind" is that so many never run long enough using their first wind to find out they have a "second wind" and never use their stamina and courage to push forward in spite of difficulties. I am told that a marathon runner at some point runs up against a physical and psychological wall; it is when they push past this point that their "second wind" kicks in and they are able to complete the race.   How did this happen? Somewhere in the past a parent, teacher, coach, or friend encouraged them to achieve regardless of the difficulties they may face. It was the development of a winning attitude and the awareness they were part of a larger group; that they had family and friends cheering them on toward the finish line. They endure because they had trained and developed a mindset to persevere; that is, to persist in an undertaking in spite of opposition, or discouragement. They used both their walking and running muscles and called on the previously developed stamina to push ahead.

Deeper Strength

Achievers and overcomers develop the same attitude as the young boy being pursued by a wild animal in the dark woods. As he grew weary he prayed, "God if you will pick up my feet, I will put them down!" He was willing to do all he could to outlast the problem. Sometimes when physical weariness overwhelms us, it is necessary to call on your deeper strength and a higher power for assistance in the race. The ancient Prophet wrote that some could "run and not grow weary, and walk and not faint."   It appears that the concept of two sets of muscles and the construct of the "second wind" have been around for a while.   Seniors must use all their muscles and keep a positive attitude to age gracefully and enjoy the journey. Using these tools could produce a Silver Lining in the next cloudy day.

Erikson's Seventh Stage of Life

The main concern of Erikson's seventh stage of development took place between ages 40 and 65. His effort was to describe a self-contained ability to create, generate, or produce new content relative to living a useful life and how this provided a positive attitude about the future. During these twenty-five years, adults normally attempt to create or nurture things that will exist beyond their death. They often see this in their children or other positive social changes generated by their efforts. This stage of life, Erikson assumed, had to do with an individual's self-contained ability to create, generate, or produce new things that benefited future generations or in other words "making one's mark" on the world. During this period, what was done to contribute to society, Erikson called "generativity." In this concept, Erikson saw an individual having an independent ability to create, generate, or produce new content for a better life.

Others who feel they did not make a significant contribution to the betterment of society in the broad fields of family and relationships, work and society generally feel a sense of "stagnation." This psychological stage referred to a sense of failure to contribute and some individuals because of this feeling may become unproductive and disconnected with reality. This further complicates the ageing process for them, their families, and those who care for them during the ageing process.

Looking Back

Looking back over this stage produces either happiness with what was created or sadness over things left undone. When looking back causes difficulty, one must look forward to the future. The twenty-five years between 40 and 65 cannot be relived. They are behind us, the only thing one can do is understand how and why they feel the way they do after age 65. This will inform what Erickson called integrity vs. despair.

Integrity vs. Despair

Erickson's last stage, **Integrity vs. Despair**, occurred during late adulthood. This is the time when individuals look back and evaluate their lives. If the previous stages developed properly, they will experience honesty, honor, and reliability. This produces what he called "integrity." If previous stages have not developed in a positive way, some may feel a kind of hopelessness and depression will follow. Some may call this "despair." Erickson assumed adult development was primarily qualitative because changes came in stages, but also quantitative as one's "identity" became stronger as their convictions solidify. He assumed that nature determines the sequence of the stages and sets the limits within which adult development operates. However, all must pass through one stage before entering the next in the stated order. Now, this is the ninth inning, and your team has two outs. The bases are loaded and you are up to bat. You can change the score; you can win! Become a champion, score some points, and win the game!

Identity and Value

Over time individuals develop both a theology and a philosophy and these combine to determine their identity that is worked out in their social roles. The combining of these two major aspects also determines their ideology, which was worked out in creative ideas and the things they valued. These facts do not disappear just because one grows older. They still think in terms of their identity and their social roles. Also, they have developed over time a system of thinking about creative ideas and values. As one ages, they wish to retain both their identity and social roles also their system that values life and creativity. Most seniors will never be satisfied to just play games, watch television, or chat on a phone with family and friends. They want to be productive and demonstrate their worth and value. It may be to draw a picture, play a tune, recite a poem, sing a song, catch a fish, or tell a funny story. Those who care for seniors must understand these facts or there will be great disappointment for all concerned. (See the list of senior achievements in Chapter One)

The Doctor was a Resident

I am reminded of an academic who was primarily a counselor and as he aged it became necessary to go to an eldercare facility. His wife understood his identity and his value system so she asked the home to rent her an extra room at the facility. She placed a desk, books, and chairs and made it similar to the office where her husband had worked for years. As long as he was able, he would rise, shower, dress, and go to his office. He would only leave the office for meals. Since he was a kind and gentle man, residents of the facility would walk into his office for a "session" with the Doctor. It was good conversation and both the Counselor and the visitor benefited from the interaction. After all, the man had two masters degrees and two doctorates in the counseling field. Even as he aged, he was capable of being of assistance. He could no longer drive a car or ride a bus, but he could walk down the hall to his office and chat with friends. It was the best arrangement that could be made under the circumstance. Each family and senior living facility should make room for meaningful participation by residents in the ongoing operation and programs of the home. This can be the Silver Lining to the clouds that hang heavily over the elderly.

Quality Counts!

Life must be something more than long. It is quality, not quantity that really counts in the long run. Being healthy and active are two of life's greatest assets. Don't tiptoe forward, embrace the ageing process. This is the best way to remain both healthy and happy. Most adults seek a good life during the final decade of life. It can be difficult to make quality decisions about this process. Everyone in the family has a part in the emotional health of seniors. If the choice is to remain healthy and happy in your home or move to assisted care, include the family in the decision. If you remain in your home, you may need assistance with meal preparation, errands, light housekeeping, transportation, laundry, companionship, and personal hygiene. Maintain your independence as long as possible. Anticipating the financial burden of ageing is vital to both health and happiness. Can you imagine retirement without financial worries?

A Good Example

A graduate student's rationale for going back to school at 68 is an example of a positive and proactive attitude about the next five years of life. He was concerned about his future and legacy. He wanted to write a book about his life and work to pass on what he had learned to the next generation. Earning a Doctor of Philosophy at 73, he projected a five year life-plan with a budget. At 78, he made another five year plan. At 83, he made another five year plan. He died twenty years after enrolling in the doctoral program, still working in a small town. His wife sent the balance of his 5-year life-plan budget to the library of his graduate school. The **DePartee Reading Room** in the library honors his understanding that the next five years were important. This has become a constant example to those working on their future. Sunrise tomorrow is an important starting point for the rest of life.

Sunrise Starts the Next 5-Years

The concern to make the next years productive is deep within the human soul and this attribute manifests itself as conscious thought, feeling, and resolve in the life of most adults. This book is an effort to explain how the declining years could be the ascending years. Each 5-year period could be the most productive and provide a valued legacy. The big question is when do the next 5-years start? The best answer at "sunrise tomorrow." With the proper attitude and opportunity, the elderly may use all the knowledge and experience gained in life to make the next years productive and meaningful by asking three questions each morning:

What can I do better?

What can I do different?

What can I do new?

An Obvious Obligation

Care and honor for elderly parents is an obvious obligation and is clearly supported by sacred writings as a moral obligation. Yet, when one chooses to neglect the needs of children, they will most likely abandon the child's mother, and ultimately neglect the care of their own elderly parents. Sacred writings are clear, adult children owe a debt of honor to their parents and this includes both respect (to look at and pay attention to), and tribute, which is a payback or a "duty or obligation" for the investment in time and energy parents made in the long-term care of their family. Now it is pay-back time.

Pay-back for Upbringing

An adult offspring could never repay parents for the cost of feeding, clothing, housing and educating them. It is responsible behavior and a positive pay-back to care for elderly parents. In Jewish times, thankless adults often placed extra funds in a kind of savings arrangement with the Temple to avoid using the money for their parents. Then when the parents passed, they would retrieve their savings and use it for themselves. It may be different now, but the attitude and action is similar in many areas when one observes the elderly and ignores their needs. This happens in spite of the prosperity of their children and the community. To neglect the elderly is a travesty in a moral society. There are always consequences when one violates such a universal guideline. When some cultures honor the elderly, it is shameful that seniors are neglected in some communities.

Planning Improves Life

The planning process will provide hope and anticipation for the day and assist with a positive attitude about life and the future. Ageing can truly have a Silver Lining when one remains optimistic and hopeful. Attitude and action based on advance planning are vital to a hopeful future. Follow the unwritten advice of an elderly gentleman, "Never retire. When you get tired doing nothing you can't stop and rest. This is why old folks die." Keep active and remain independent as long as you can. When the time comes that you must depend on others for essential things, be grateful for what you have. Old age is a blessing that many do not experience. Meanwhile, turn over a few rocks.

Turn Over a few Rocks

There is a story of an elderly social worker traveling in a third world country. As she walked along a path, she would repeatedly venture out a few steps and turn over a rock or two. When a companion asked, "Why do you turn over rocks?" Her response was clear, "I want things to be different because I was here, so I turn over a few rocks. It may be a small thing, but this way I am sure to make some changes along the path I traveled. I may not change the world, but others will know I made an effort to change things along this path."

Have you made your mark on the world? Could you turn over a few more rocks along the path so others will know the way you traveled? Will you be remembered? How far did you venture from the pathway to turn over a rock or two? What did you find? One fellow said, "I just turned over that rock and now I clearly understand how things work." How's that, asked a friend. "Well, a few ants were working hard and seem to be doing all the work, while all the rest were scattering in panic." Were you among the workers that made a difference or one who scattered in fright? Is this what you found during your life journey? Perhaps so; therefore, you must turn over a few more rocks along the pathway. You have miles to go before you sleep. Keep pushing you can make a difference. Pass on your wisdom to the next generation, so others will know you traveled this way and made a difference. It may be small, but you can make a difference. Be proud of each accomplishment. The world, your community, your family, and your friends are blessed because you passed this way. Face the future with confidence, the world is a better place because of you.

The "Mental" Immune System

When the gas tank is low in a vehicle, a little gauge shows the driver the need to stop for petrol, but the vehicle continues to run as usual. Why? Because the driver knows the tank is "low" not "empty" and that the engine will still run and move the vehicle forward. The gauge does not turn off the engine, because the driver remains in control. Normally, it is the decision of the driver to view the problem and continue the journey until additional fuel is available and the tank is filled for the rest of the journey. Would it not be foolish to park the car on the side of the road and remain there with fuel still in the tank? It is the same when one feels low, but knows they can continue forward. Parking on the sidelines when a problem occurs and having a "pity party" does not solve the problem. Recognize the problem, continue on the journey, find a place to "fill the tank" and not become sidetracked or hindered from reaching your destination. Doing this strengthens the mental immune system that permits you to recognize a problem and not let it control your forward movement. You are the driver; you are in charge of your life.   Solvable problems should not sidetrack you or cause you to be parked in a place you don't want to be. Permit your mental immune system to work and assist your decision making when a difficulty exists. You have personal worth and value, there is still fuel in the tank! Keep moving ahead.

Fuel for the Journey

Thinking about the absence of something good could enable you to be grateful for what you have. What if you had never met your friends, your spouse, your family? If you did not exist, what kind of life would your loved ones have? Do you remember Frank Capra's film, *It's a Wonderful Life?* George Bailey, with support from an Angel, learned the difficult life his family and friends would have had without him. The tank may be low, but there is still fuel enough to keep moving ahead. Also, there is a place ahead to fill the tank that will bring you fresh fuel for the journey. A difficult experience strengthens your mental immune system and develops coping skills needed to deal with the rainy days of life. Feelings of gratitude for fuel in the tank could strengthen your problem solving system and lessen the impact of a negative experience. There is wisdom in this proverb, "It's better to have loved and lost than never to have loved at all." Could it be that learning lessons from problems provides fresh fuel for the journey and enables you to handle rainy days?

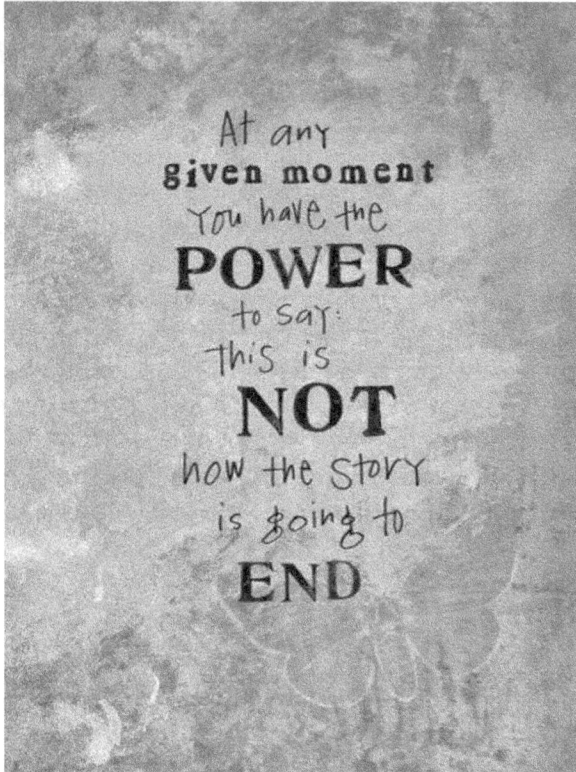

At any
given moment
You have the
POWER
to say:
This is
NOT
how the Story
is going to
END

10

COPING

WITH RAINY DAYS

Rainy Days and Bad Situations

What does it mean to cope with the rainy days and the other blue or black days of life? The concept of coping comes from the Latin meaning "raincoat" and suggests advance plans for dealing with the normal and recurring bad times in every life. In architecture coping is the covering of a wall with a slanting top to shed water; also coping is to lay a protective top course of a wall to keep it from eroding. Coping is the process of managing actual emotional and stressful situations. Coping is also a long ceremonial cape used in performing normal acts of worship for those seeking a safe harbor from the cares of life. Using the knowledge and experience gained throughout life, mature adults can construct a wall that sheds the rain, protects the things they value, assists in many stressful situations, and seek personal security and sanctuary to make the last decades of life constructive and meaningful. This should be the objective of all involved in eldercare!

Lessons Learned

The best way to get through the dark days is to start by being thankful for the life you have. A little gratitude goes a long way in overcoming a bad experience and assisting positive steps forward. There once was a man who believed that everything in his life was preordained by a higher power. One day he made a false step, stumbled and fell and as he was getting up whispered, "Thank God, that's over." Well, you may not think the same way, but when a bad experience is "over," get "over" it as quickly as possible. Mature individuals learn to identify and appreciate the lessons learned from regretful events by asking "What could I learn from this experience? How could I behave differently in the future? Did my behavior create this situation?"

The Next Raindrop

Coping is expending conscious effort to solve both personal and interpersonal problems and seeking to minimize stress or conflict in daily living. Yet, when the rain stops and a ray of sunlight shines through the vanishing clouds, hope springs eternal in the human heart. This produces *euphoria*, positive expectation, genuine optimism, intense happiness, and the increased ability to cope with daily trials. Coping skills develop over time as they are utilized to improve one's attitude and action to respond positively to the ups-and-downs of normal living situations. This positive attitude prepares one to feel the next raindrop without despair and fear that a Noah-type flood is coming that will wash away everything of value. There may be an occasional deluge and even a rare flash flood, but the new coping "raincoat" will assist most adults in handling future difficulties in a mature manner. This will smooth the way forward to a wonderful life.

Life, Lessons and Legacy

Portraits are hung, statues and memorials are erected for the world's heroic figures and foremost dignitaries, but these monuments normally express only a snapshot of a life: not the heritage they passed to children, grandchildren, friends, and neighbors. We see a man on a horse and understand he was a heroic and noble figure, but we learn little about his life and family. We visit a memorial park and see the colorful flowers and beautiful greenery, but we learn little about the real person honored by the marvelous garden. We only know the person had dignity or wealth and left a material legacy for others. Even modern heroes are honored for a specific event that saved a life or demonstrated a self-sacrifice that benefited others, but we still know little about the person or their life. We honor a sports figure for action in a single game without knowing anything about their morals, ethics or lifestyle. No one should be judged or honored for a single act; it is the whole of life that counts. What lessons did their daily lives teach us? What example of living can we follow? What deep memories of their way of life found a place in our hearts and minds? Did they leave a living legacy? Were they moral examples for others to follow?

Hardships and Happiness

There was no park or monument built for Rosie, but she was a wonderful woman. Perhaps every son thinks his mother was the greatest, especially after she is gone. Looking back on the eighty-six (86) years that Rosie Latchmin Ramjattan lived, I am no exception. With clear recall, Mama is remembered as being happy even during hardship days. Rain or shine she was ready to assist her family and others in need. Her greatest regret was not being able to help some when they needed assistance. Mama was always ready and willing to share her lessons of grace and charity with her children and others in the village. Her famous words, "Never look down at someone unless you are willing to help them get up" implanted a desire in me to assist the disadvantaged. She was a sister, a wife, mother of ten, great cook, good seamstress, fair shopkeeper, community banker, post mistress, community worker, teacher, and a woman who practiced her faith. She, together with my father, taught many life lessons that have been lived out in the daily lives and professions of her family. Some of these are recorded in the book, *The Anapausis Partnership* (2011). Yet the book did not chronicle the specifics of Mama's life, lessons, and legacy being shared as a tribute in this volume. (See **Appendix Five**.)

Coping with Rainy Days

When Mama operated a small shop, she served as a kind of "village banker" for those who often had more month than money. Rather than giving credit to villagers, she would ask for money in advance and keep the money in personalized envelopes for their future needs. When they needed stuff from the shop, she would "withdraw" from their personal "account envelop." This taught a worthy lesson to the poor who often spent all their money and had nothing left for the rainy days. According to Michelle, a granddaughter, Rosie was "a great humanitarian," because she always sought to improve the lives of others.

Positive View of the Future

Mama cared deeply about the children of Plum Mitan, a rural agricultural village on the eastern seaboard of Trinidad and Tobago. She saw the children of the village as future productive citizens. Mama even operated a rice mill as a needed service for the village. She always looked to the future and even planned for the ageing process. Mama practiced writing with her left hand just in case her right hand failed, because she loved to write letters of encouragement. She taught her children by word and example to set their eyes on what they could become, rather than on who they were at the moment. Mama was a good seamstress and made clothes for herself, the family and others. She actually made the dress in which she was buried. Mama was a woman of simple faith and regularly made sacrifices for her family and community. Her positive view of the future made her life a living lesson for us all.

Passed Kindness Forward

Mama never let her personal disappointments spill over into the lives of others. She practiced what she taught others, even in the midst of hardships and always attempted to remain happy and active. Rosie was a strong woman and did not show her personal struggles to others. Perhaps this inner beauty came from the flowers her mother used to name her and her sisters: Rosie, Lilly, and Daisy. These three made a beautiful bouquet with a fragrance that lingers beyond their lifespan. Rosie Ramjattan's legacy was that she passed kindness to everyone during her sojourn on earth as an example for others to follow. A few lines from a poem seem to be appropriate parting words from Mama:

"So when tomorrow starts without me,
Don't think we're far apart,
For every time you think of me,
I'm right there, in your heart!"

(See Appendix Five)

Action and Attitude

Regardless of how one copes with living, to facilitate a hopeful future, one must develop a positive outlook on life to have a chance at survival. Since **attitude** and **action** are closely related, *attitude being a predisposition to action.* It would be helpful if the elderly and their caregivers understood the need for action that can change attitudes. Changing one's mind does not change things; action is required to change attitudes. For example, when one awakes early and still feels tired and sleepy, just thinking about the situation does not change events. Action, however, such as, getting out of bed, taking a shower, dressing for the day, will change the predisposition to act. After this positive activity, no one thinks or feels that it would be wise to go back to bed for a long sleep. Why? Now they are ready to face the day with a positive attitude. This can produce meaningful achievement.

Action and Achievement

Action is necessary for achievement. Purposeful activities can move the elderly toward achievement. All eldercare givers must provide activities and actions that can change the attitude of the elderly and move them in a positive direction. Otherwise, they will simple remain in bed and waste the day. This would be a terrible waste of intellect and expertise that is badly needed in a troubled world. This achievement may only be getting out of bed and dressing for the day or it could be the beginning of a creative contribution to society. Caregivers must never forget that all of previous living prepares one for the remainder of life. All that happens in the past relates to the present and the future. Each caregiver must squeeze the last ounce of action out the elderly; that is, the elderly must see themselves as having ability to produce something worthwhile. If a farmer wants milk, he doesn't take a stool to the pasture and wait for a cow to back up for milking. The fisherman doesn't expect the fish to jump into his boat. One must think, plan, and organize to achieve.

Action and Happiness

In fact, action is the process of doing something in order to achieve a purpose, objective or goal. Worthwhile lessons are learned from productive people. Those who whistle the tune of "do nothing or do little" and actually "do less," may only become a little more than a "good-bad" example. Action may not bring happiness, but there is no happiness without action. When one believes that life is worth living, positive action will follow. The elderly can alter their lives by changing their daily activities. A failure to achieve can breed dissatisfaction, discontent, and disease. A feeling of general discomfort or uneasiness may be overcome with positive behavior. With lessons learned from the past, cloudy weather or rainy days will only be a temporary setback. The crucial and decisive action will be ongoing and will influence a positive lifestyle. Both faith and action are required to function in spite of rainy days.

Carry an Umbrella

This old story comes out of the rural countryside. It seems a long drought had caused great loss of crops and livestock and the rural parson called for a prayer meeting. Several gathered at the old country church, but only one man and the parson brought an umbrella. Upon observation, the parson asked all but the man who brought the umbrella to go home. "Me and this brother with the umbrella will stay and pray for rain!" The moral of this story: if you pray for rain carry an umbrella. In other words, one needs both hope and expectancy to produce the works that faith requires.

Burning Daylight

An old saying of farmers and labor-intensive workers was "We are burning daylight." This had the meaning that one must work during the daylight hours because the night is coming when there is no light to work. Life's journey is similar to this construct. During the various stages of life, one must work while they can and do what can be done because changes are coming. The force of continued change cannot be held back by the will, all must work within the framework of time and time is short. There are no guarantees of a tomorrow; in fact, it is always tomorrow and tomorrow never arrives. One saying described tomorrow "as the day we worried about yesterday." Why worry, be happy and do what you can; that is all you can do. There is no reason for regrets about things left undone. We all burn up too much daylight and often leave unfinished business.

Unfinished Business

Did you hear about the cowboy who saddled his horse backward so he could see where he had been? Well he discovered he could not see where he was going. Living in the past is a bad place to be, but denying events of the past could be a worse place to live.

Things in the past that caused emotional distress will never bring present peace unless they are revisited. The best plan is to revisit the situation to bring clarity to the issues and deal with them. Otherwise you will always be dealing with unfinished business. Dealing with broken promises, unfulfilled commitments, or unsolved relationship issues can produce guilt, grief, and depression. Deal with these in person if possible, if not, write a letter, or seek forgiveness from a higher power if distance or death robs you of a face-to-face possibility. Do not live with unfinished business.

Advance Planning Demonstrates Faith

To have hope for a desired outcome one must have both desire and faith: if you do not have both you will have fear. In fact, if you want something to happen, but do not believe it will happen, you have fear that it will not occur. Otherwise, if you believe something will happen, but you do not want it to happen, you are fearful that it will happen. The umbrella showed advance planning that included both desire and faith; they wanted rain and expected rain so they brought an umbrella. This is what the family of seniors must do: have hope in the future. What do you want and what do you expect to happen? Plan where they will live out your last days. Will it be alone at the family home? Will they move in with a son or daughter and share their home with children? Will the senior need special care? What can the family afford? Will you need an eldercare facility? Planning in advance is similar to carrying an umbrella when you expect it to rain. Planning for senior care requires more than a "piggy bank" and a map. There are many options and decisions should be made before there is a family emergency. When there is an agreed-on plan, when the time comes, the planning can provide a Silver Lining to the cloudy days of ageing and eldercare.

Some Plans don't Work

Whether the plans were made by mice or men, they often do not work out as expected.   In the poem about a mouse by Robert Burns, he describes how a mouse built a home thought to be indestructible but was destroyed by a farmer's plow. Sometimes the planned way forward becomes a twisted and impossible path to travel. Anyone who has read Steinbeck's novel based on "the best laid plans of mice and men" clearly understand that plans do not always follow our wishes. Perhaps at times what we considered plans were just "dreams" and one cannot write an agenda for a dream. A dream is often a fantasy or an unreal thought. Real plans have objectives and goals and a list of procedures in order of priority. What to do first, second, etc. The reason some "plans" fail is that there was no agenda and no priority order for procedural steps to achieve the goals and objectives. What is the answer? Make better plans with logical and practical steps. Follow a developed plan relative to the end of life issues. This structure for the end of life issues can bring peace to the process and assist the terminally ill with a smooth passage into the afterlife.

Relevant End of Life Suggestions

Here are relevant end of life suggestions from an experienced Nurse, Mrs. Wayne E. Faust, who worked decades with the elderly and observed many dying patients. She used these ideas in her personal life and in counseling with clients who needed support in handling their feelings when it became necessary to approach the death of a loved one. "I have seen the following thoughts in action and the process offered peace to most parties involved." When you approach the death of a loved one or a close friend, use these simple suggestions. The earthly life is not over until their personal song is finished. Be patient!

> ► **Accept** that you do not need to be an official faith-based leader or medical staff to serve the needs of the dying person; it is natural human behavior.

> ► **Give** YOURSELF permission to release the person who needs to complete their earthly journey.

> ► **Remind** the dying person of some gifts you have received in sharing his/her life.

> ► **Share** a memory by saying, "I remember when" rather than asking "Do you remember when?"

> ► **Assure** the dying person that all their loved ones will be alright.

> ► **Give** your spoken permission to release the patient to complete their earthly journey.

> ► **Encourage** others to give their permission for the person to make the transition into the afterlife.

> ► **Speak** aloud the names of other "loved ones" that are "waiting on the other side."

> ► **Offer** thanksgiving for the patient's life and for the privilege of sharing this transition experience.

> ► **Sit** quietly for a few minutes. If possible, touch the person and softly sing, recite a favorite song or play a recording if you are unable to personally do this.

> ► **Tell** the patient "I am leaving the room for a few minutes, but I will be back soon."

► **These steps may need to be softly and tenderly repeated** several times over a period of hours, days, months. Death is a process, not an event. Please see this transition experience as an opportunity to share time with a special person.

—Susanne Faust, RN, MLitt, CSAC

(Used by permission)

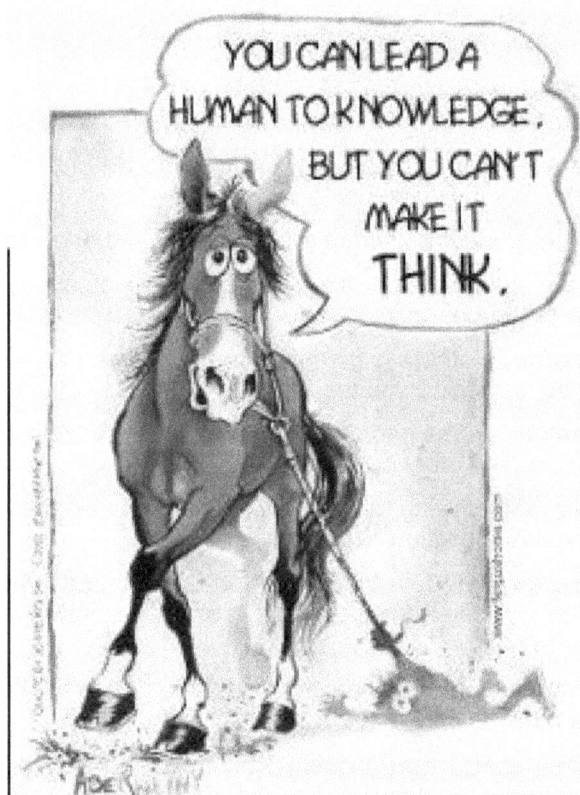

AFTERWORD

geing Has a Silver Lining is both an unusual and useful book which contains the distillate of practical experience and reflection. It has universal appeal and is based on the fact that every thinking and reflective reader will learn something from the experience of a wise and perceptive guide who is travelling the same pathway to the inevitable *terminus ad quo --"the end from which the beginning starts."* Here will be found sound practical advice for every dimension of life – physical, spiritual, and psychological. The result is a book that will serve as a useful roadmap which will result in benefits accruing to the reader's physical health, diet, exercise, the spiritual dimension, social relatedness and indeed to every aspect of the journey of life.

The reader will participate in the race of life and will be exposed to the fascinating perceptions of one who reflects on the various stages in the journey. When the last lap of this passage is reached or is approaching, thoughts of the past steps taken and decisions made will tend to flood the consciousness and here the author shares his personal experiences and lessons learned.

Ageing Has a Silver Lining is a mind stretching must read for everyone who is aware of the race in which she or he is participating and who recognizes that the golden years are just around the corner. The knowledge gained will go a long way in preventing those precious years from degenerating into the rusty years. The author demonstrates that he is a keen and accurate observer of *la condition humaine* and has successfully distilled his perceptions, reflections, recommendations, and conclusions for all of us who are engaged in the perennial search for beacons along the undulating vicissitudes of life. The result of consideration of the wisdom expressed by this author will help all of us achieve the Roman adage, *bis vivit qui bene vivit*, "he who lives well lives twice."

— **E. Basil Jackson, MD, PhD, JD** *Distinguished Professor of Psychiatry, Medicine, and Law*

Appendices

Appendix One
Changes that Occur with Age

Appendix Two
Effects of Aging on Physical Structure

Appendix Three
Healthy Eating for Seniors

Appendix Four
A Checklist for Application for Residency

Appendix Five
In Memory of Rosie Ramjattan

Appendix Six
Risk Assessment for Positive Aging

Appendix Seven
Senior Attitudes about Staying Active

Appendix Eight
Know the Warning Signs
A Final Warning

If YOU HAVE A LOVING FAMILY, A FEW GOOD FRIENDS, FOOD ON YOUR TABLE, AND A ROOF OVER YOUR HEAD, YOU ARE RICHER THAN YOU THINK!

Appendix One

Changes that Occur with Age

As the ageing process moves forward everyone notices changes. Some obvious changes are:

- Bruises appear more often.
- Changes in nails and skin appear.
- Constipation increases.
- Eliminate becomes urgent.
- Heart pumps less.
- It becomes harder to rise and shine.
- Memory function slows a little.
- More aches and pains.
- Most become a little shorter.
- Personal hygiene becomes more difficult.
- Recovery time from injury increases.
- Sexual expression changes.
- Teeth become a problem.
- Walking slows.
- Weight gain seems automatic.

I Can Rise And Shine, Just Not At The Same Time.

Appendix Two

Effects of Aging on Physical Structure

Gerontologists study the social and behavioral effects of aging. The biological effects of aging, such as the loss of flexibility in some tissues and the decline of organ function, can influence these social and behavioral effects. For example, the heart becomes less efficient as a person ages, making exercise more difficult.

Organ or System	Natural Effects of Aging	Accelerating Factors
Skin	Loses thickness and elasticity (wrinkles appear)	Process accelerated by smoking, excessive exposure to sun
	Bruises more easily as blood vessels near surface weaken	
Brain/Nervous System	Loses some capacity for memorization and learning as cells die	Process accelerated by overuse of alcohol and other drugs, repeated blows to the head
	Becomes slower to respond to stimuli (reflexes dull)	
Senses	Become less sharp with loss of nerve cells	Process accelerated by smoking, repeated exposure to loud noise
Lungs	Become less efficient as elasticity decreases	Process accelerated by smoking, poor air quality, insufficient exercise
Heart	Pumps less efficiently, making exercise more difficult	Process accelerated by overuse of alcohol and tobacco, poor eating habits
Circulation	Worsens, and blood pressure rises, as arteries harden	Process accelerated by injury, obesity
Joints	Lose mobility (knee, hip) and deteriorate from constant wear and pressure (disappearance of cartilage between vertebrae results in old age 'shrinking')	Process accelerated by injury, obesity
Muscles	Lose bulk and strength	Process accelerated by insufficient exercise, starvation
Liver	Filters toxins from blood less efficiently	Process accelerated by alcohol abuse, viral infection

Appendix Three

Healthy Eating for Seniors

An excellent 214 page handbook, Healthy *Eating for Seniors,* is a guide for the nourishment and care for seniors. A free download at **http://www.healthlinkbc.ca/healthyeating/ stages/seniors.html**

CONTENTS

- Breakfast and snacks:
- Sunny Orange Shake,
- Pumpkin Raisin Muffins, Fruit Lax

- **Lunch or Dinner:**
Herbed Lentil and Barley Soup,
Spinach Salad with Orange Seed Dressing, Broccoli Salad,
Tuna Garden, Tofu Stir-Fry, Quick Steamed Fish Fillets with
Potatoes and Asparagus, Skillet Pork Chops with Sweet
Potatoes and Couscous, Meatloaf, Indian Curry Sauté,
Spinach Frittata, Sweet & Sour Chicken and Vegetable
Casserole, Beef, Vegetable and Pasta Casserole

- **Desserts:**
  Quick Fruit Compote, Berry Cobbler, Fresh Fruit and Nut
  Desserts

- **Extras:** Universal Seasoning, Salt-Free Vinaigrette Salad
  Dressing

Appendices:

Appendix Four

A Checklist for Application for Residency

Possible Intake Data or Personal Information Needed by an Eldercare Facility; such as, for Olive's House

Personal Information Needed

Date of Birth _____/_____/_____

Place of Birh_____

Citizenship_____

Name _____

Address_____

Religion_____

Primary Physician_____

Next of Kin _____

Contact Numbers for the above _____

Important Records And Documents Required

Yes / No   Location Stored / Need to Locate

Savings Accounts _____

Checking Accounts_____

CD's _____

Stocks_____

Bonds _____

Mutual Funds_____

Notes_____

Real estate_____

Valuable Objects_____

Home Owner Insurance_____

Car insurance_____

Life insurance_____

Long Term Care Ins ._____

Funeral Insurance_____

Other insurance_____

Credit Cards _____

Mortgages_____

Vehicle Titles_____

Charitable Donations_____

Tax Records_____

Deeds to Property_____

Health Care Records_____

Birth Certificate_____

Marriage Certificate_____

Will_____

Medical POA _____

Financial POA_____

Living Will_____

Advanced Directives_____

Funeral Preferences _____

Safety Deposit Box_____

Important Contact Names And Numbers

Family: Children _____

_____

_____

_____

Grandchildren:_____

_____

Religious Leader: _____

Neighbors:_____

_____

Friends_____

_____

It would assist Olive's House with your care if the staff knew the things you enjoy doing including your trade skills and primary work specialization. The more the staff knows about your past interest, the easier it will be for them to plan your participation in activities you enjoy.

Sports and Entertainment Interests

What sports did you enjoy the most?_____

_____

What kind of games do you enjoy playing? _____

_____

Do you enjoy Television? What kind of programs _____

_____

Do you enjoy video or movies? ( ) Yes ( ) No

Do you enjoy listening to music? ( ) Yes ( ) No

If so, what kind of music?_____

_____

Do you play a musical instrument? ( ) Yes ( ) No Which one:_____

_____

Do you enjoy singing? ( ) Yes ( ) No

Do you appreciate opportunities to attend a religious service? ( ) Yes ( ) No

Do you enjoy reading? ( ) Yes ( ) No

To help us build Olive's House Lbrary, what kind of books do you enjoy?_____

_____

_____

Do you enjoy just talking with others? ( ) Yes ( ) No

Do you enjoy walking and seeing nature? ( ) Yes ( ) No

Do you enjoy a ride in the country side? ( ) Yes ( ) No

Do you enjoy going to the beach? ( ) Yes ( ) No

SKILLS INVENTORY AND WORK HISTORY -- How would you classify your work experience, work skills, or work specialization? Check those that best describe your talent and primary work:

[ ] Accounting

[ ] Administration

[ ] Building/Construction

[ ] Business

[ ] Childcare

[ ] Computers/ Communication

[ ] Counselling

[ ] Early Childhood Education

[ ] Electrician

[ ] Finance/Banking

[ ] Government worker

[ ] Homemaker

[ ] Law/Law Enforcement/Security

[ ] Management

[ ] Marketing

[ ] Mason

[ ] Music

[ ] Plumber

[ ] Religious worker

[ ] Sales

[ ] Social Worker

[ ] Teacher Primary level

[ ] Teacher Secondary level

[ ] Teacher Tertiary level

[ ] Other skills or work knowledge not listed above:_____

_____

_____

_____

_____

_____

_____

_____

If there is anything else you would want the staff to know about you and your life experiance:_____

_____

_____

_____

_____

_____

Appendix Five

In Memory of

Rosie Ramjattan

The life of Rosie Ramjattan fulfilled the Sacred Words recorded by Saint Paul: "Practice sharing the heavy burdens of others and you will fulfill the law of Christ." What did Rosie Ramjattan learn from being a wife, mother of 10, great cook, good seamstress, fair shopkeeper, community banker, post mistress, community worker, teacher, and a woman who practiced carrying the heavy burdens of others?

Rosie learned when you carry the burdens of others; they must be unloaded. One must never hold on to a heavy burden, but must find a time and place to unload that burden. Rosie learned to cast her burdens on God. She would want you to do the same. Of course, you are saddened by her passing, but there is no sorrow that heaven cannot heal. Today we share our burden and they seem less heavy.

Rosie learned patience to bear up under the normal burdens of life. Life was not easy for her, as wife with limited income. Many things needed by a family cannot be purchased on meager income of a hard-working man. So she opened a small store to help with family needs and assist others in need. She learned from her husband's old truck that on a hard climb, when the load was heavy, you can always downshift and climb that difficult hill. This was a good life lesson. When the load is heavy and the road is rough and steep…we should exercise patience and just downshift to a lower gear to get more power and make the journey a little easier.

Rosie learned that there are hills and valleys in life, ups and downs, peace and sorrow. Yet, she learned that a burden shared was half as heavy and a blessing shared was twice as nice. This she did this even to her last days speaking with a smile with family and friends, and with a good attitude she helped others with their ups and downs.

Rosie learned to save and share. Even as a young woman with the proceeds from her "little store" she helped others who were less fortunate.

It is time for those who remain to step up and take over the "Load Bearing Business" and participate in the "save and share" example established by Rosie Ramjattan. During the past few days I have tried to think what she would want to say to family and friends gathered here today:

"If tomorrow starts without me,
And I'm not there to see,
If the sun should rise and find your eyes
all filled with tears for me;
I wish so much you wouldn't cry
the way you did today,
While thinking of the many things,
We didn't get to say.

I know how much you love me,
As much as I love you,
And each time that you think of me,
I know you'll miss me too;
But when tomorrow starts without me,
Please try to understand,
that an angel came and called my name,
And took me by the hand,
And said my place was ready,
In heaven far above,
And that I'd have to leave behind
all those I dearly love.

But when I walked through heaven's gates,
I felt so much at home.
When God looked down and smiled at me,

From His great golden throne,
He said, "This is eternity,
And all I've promised you."
Today your life on earth is past,
but here life starts anew.
I promise no tomorrow,
But today will always last,
and since each day is the same way,
There's no longing for the past.

David M. Romano

The final verse of this poem was placed on her Funeral Notice:

"So when tomorrow starts without me,
don't think we're far apart,
For every time you think of me,
I'm right there, in your heart!"

Risk Assessment for Positive Aging

(Used by permission)

Positive healthy living requires proactive and creative assessments of the risks to that lifestyle. This risk assessment seeks to provide such an effort to prepare for and extend the active, healthy, and positive lifestyle as one ages. This assessment is based upon several tenets of behavior. These are:

1. All human beings are created equal, limited only by their innate potential and opportunity.

2. The individual has the right to determine what his or her needs are and how they are to be met.

3. The individual has a responsibility to one's self, their family, and to society at large.

4. All behavior has a purpose and is symptomatic of one's inner drives and strivings.

5. There is a tendency to behave the way one is expected to behave.

These tenets become essential as older individuals and those around them make plans for living life positively and to the fullest as the aging process progresses. One further note is taken from the work of Erick Ericson in his work on the stages of man. The final stage of psychosocial development requires one to look back on one's life with either a sense of integrity or despair.

Most studies in the realm of senior adult risk assessment point to self-neglect as the leading cause of difficulty in positive living in later years. Self-neglect may occur from several factors. We will look at these factors in their context. This assessment looks at three contexts in which assessment for positive outcomes occur. These contexts are his or her medical problems, functional status, and social milieu. These contexts have not been listed in order of importance. Rather they are listed in the order most frequently considered by individuals, family and friends, social support groups, and social agencies.

This assessment addresses these contexts in the order listed above. Rather than providing a checklist of items. A narrative format is provided which allows for examples when considering factors of risk on which to be focused or of which to be aware as potential circumstances or avoidable problems are creatively addressed.

Medical Circumstances

1. Physical health and mental status become the first realm at which we look. These elements are the usual, and sadly the only factors considered in determining steps for positive aging. Some medical conditions are acute. Sore throats, colds, flu, and such easily cared for conditions, but the elderly should consider shots for shingles, influenza and pneumonia.

Some medical problems are chronic and need regular consultations with physicians, nurses, and other professional caregivers, such as physical therapists, nutritionists, and behavioral counselors. Some factors require palliative or comfort care. These run the gamut of stiff and sore muscles to arthritis and such disorders.

Other factors to consider beyond these common elements of aging may include the sensory perception of the individual. Differentiating between colors or color blindness may prevent someone from being burned on a red hot element of a stove. Other ways of determining whether a stove-top eye or oven is on may be appropriate. The same applies for wall installed heating elements and space heaters.

Loss of taste has ruined many meals and made the person seem to become confused. When people who cook to taste lose their sense of "saltiness," for instance, more and more salt may be added to the point the food is overly salty and friends and family think "Mama is having problems with confusion. She forgot she had already salted the beans and used more salt."

Problems may occur due to loss of hearing. When men begin to lose hearing, they first lose the higher pitched tones. Women tend to lose the lower or bass tones. When women perceive, as an example, that husbands are not hearing or not listening, or need to be heard over a blaring television, they tend to raise their voices and shout. This, of course, elevates the pitch of their voice, making them even less likely to be heard.

Loss of the sense of touch may occur with diabetic periphery neuropathy, the loss of feeling in feet, legs, and fingers due to nerve damage. Sensible shoes can help resolve that problem and wearing them in the house rather than going barefoot is recommended. It may be desirable to have an "inside pair of shoes" and an "outside pair of shoes," to protect carpets, floors, and tiles.

Handrails inside and outside for steps is advisable to prevent falling, even if falling has yet to become a problem. Likewise, tub railings and a tub stool for bathing or showering can help prevent injuries due to falls. A railing down a long hall might also be considered.

Here is another word about falling—the breaking of the hip. When someone is determined to have a broken hip, the typical "diagnosis" is that the person has fallen. In fact, the reverse is more commonly the truth. The hip breaks and the person falls. This reinforces the need for good nutritional health and frequent physical examinations. Frequently someone may become depressed after a fall and a broken hip. Loving and well-meaning people assume that the person has become depressed because he or she realizes they are losing their independence and having some emotional issues. Not necessarily the case. In fact, more likely the physical trauma from the break has caused the depression. Much depression is caused, assuredly, by emotional stressors: fear, anger and guilt being the primary ones. However, hormonal shifts and chemical imbalances of a physical nature may cause depressive episodes. Good clinical assessment by a professional is recommended .

One final word about depression. Dr. Ross Campbell, a psychiatrist who practiced many years said that up to 50% of the people with the diagnosis of Alzheimer's disease actually do not have it; rather, they have severe forms of depression. Again a good clinical assessment is required rather than assumptions made. Working in these realms of prevention will aid in a positive process of healthy aging. This fact cannot be emphasized enough. Be attentive and look for signs of potential self-neglect.

2. Functional status goes hand-in-glove with physical, medical, and mental status. Much has already been stated regarding functional status. Just another few words about prevention as it relates to functionality. What are the functions with which a person might need assistance? Are falls an issue? Are stairs an issue? Is eyesight and the ability to read labels on prescription bottles a problem? What about alert systems for fire, smoke, home invasion, or falling. "Help, I've fallen and I can't get up" commercials should not be taken lightly, especially if one lives alone. These kinds of alert systems provide a greater sense of security for the older individual. A little expense for a greater feeling of safety and assistance when needed may provide all concerned with a greater peace of mind. Some churches and agencies have a telephone assurance program which calls individuals each day to be sure they are up and doing well for the day. Check into this option or introduce a "buddy" system with a friend.

We have covered four of the five senses: hearing, seeing, feeling or touch, and taste. A brief comment about smell. This becomes important in the refrigerator. This consideration is greater if one is losing the sense of taste. A system of dating can be implemented with masking tape and black marking pens. Strict adherence to these use-by dates can avoid several potential health risks.

3. Much can be said about the social milieu of individuals. Again we address first those living alone. These individuals are

at the greatest risk. Steps to ensure independence on a daily basis can be effective in preventing injury.

A telephone assurance program or "buddy" system is a first line of prevention. Not only does this give assurance to the individual, it provides human contact and interaction on a daily basis. For some living alone, this may be the most significant contact of the day. One reason people lose track of the day is not confusion but a lack of stimulation. Most people have watches, or check the date with the daily newspaper or an on-line service. Not everyone has that opportunity to stay oriented as to day, date, and place. These telephone assurances can be an excellent service. Keeping oriented often is just being aware.

Positive living in aging means positive relationships. Senior Centers, travel or garden clubs, social and civic activities provide needed activity, socialization, and stimulation. These activities should not be neglected. For those who do not drive, friends and neighbors can provide transportation and social interaction. Shopping for groceries can become a social activity with a friend or family member. It is about more than groceries. It helps create a positive social environment. The older person may still be capable of driving to the supermarket and purchase groceries. But this can be an opportunity for a weekly outing for family or friends.

This brief statement of risk assessment for positive living during the aging process should be considered as a starting point for the individual and for family and friends. Hopefully, this assessment begins a process of considering the physical and mental environment, the functional considerations, and the social environment for positive aging. Certainly it is not comprehensive and definitely is not a checklist. Remember, the individual must evaluate and decide what is in his or her best interest. Each person also has personal responsibility to herself or himself, to the family, and to others in the society in which they live.

— **Donald B. Smith**, MSSW, LCSW, DPhil
Board Certified Diplomate in Clinical Social Work (Aging) U.S.A.

Appendix Seven

Senior Attitudes about Staying Active

(Used by permission)

As people age, abilities and opportunities to make some decisions change, particularly about exercise and fitness.   Financial limitations, change in residency, health difficulties and transportation issues can all lead to limitations in maintaining connections. Friends, family, church, and other community groups are important for social and emotional health, and activity is important physical health. Healthcare professionals are concerned about the safety of pushing to remain connected with old lifestyle choices or even picking up new choices that require increases in mobility as an active citizen. The default reaction is to advise caution and extra care in making decisions that increase exposure to a variety of new and challenging environments.

An attitude of self-advocacy can engage the healthcare provider at the next level of consideration. When advised to cut back or redirect lifestyle choices, a key is asking the right questions. Several helpful starters are, "Under what conditions may I participate in the activity?" or "How can I modify that activity so I can continue participation?" and "Is there a better or safer environment to conduct the activity?" or "What is a good substitute to get the same benefits?"

The person asking the questions is most often in control of the meeting. Appropriate inquiry will lead the advisor to treat you as an informed client and soon-to-be more informed client. When inviting others into the decision-making circle with leading questions, not only are they forced to think more but the person asking must listen and reflect on the additional, refining Information. Personal, customized information gives the opportunity to take ownership of the present condition and direction while molding the future.

For those whose health or age will not permit aerobics, seniors will be able to obtain more information and access to a specialized exercise program. *COTHenterprises.com* will be FREE to seniors who do not have insurance coverage.

Program Developer: Bryan Thomas Phillips,
BA, MLitt, PhD (Cand.)
Environmental Science Teacher and STEM Coordinator
(Science, Technology, Engineering and Mathematics)

Appendix Eight

Know the Warning Signs

Warning Signs of a Heart Attack

Heart and blood vessel disease is a No. 1 killer. Most of the deaths from these diseases are from coronary heart disease, which includes heart attack. Many of these deaths could be prevented by acting fast at the first signs of trouble. Some heart attacks are sudden and intense, but most start slowly, with mild pain or discomfort. Here are the signs that could mean a heart attack is happening:

Chest Discomfort: Most heart attacks involve discomfort in the center of the chest that lasts more than a few minutes, or that goes away and comes back. It can feel like uncomfortable pressure, squeezing, fullness or pain.

Discomfort in Areas of The Upper Body: Symptoms can include pain or discomfort in one or both arms, the back, neck, jaw, or stomach.

Shortness of Breath: This may occur with or without chest discomfort.

Other Signs: These may include breaking out in a cold seat, nausea, or lightheadedness. The most common heart attack symptom for both men and women is chest pain or discomfort, but women are more likely than men to experience some of the other common symptoms: shortness of breath, nausea/vomiting, and back or jaw pain.

What should I do? Don't wait more than five minutes before calling a local emergency medical service, fire department, or an ambulance. If you are the one having symptoms, and you can't access emergency medical services, have someone drive you to the nearest medical facility immediately. Don't drive yourself, unless you have no other option.

What else can I do? If properly trained and it becomes necessary, give CPR (mouth-to-mouth rescue breathing and chest compressions) to a victim until help arrives. However, before thee is an emergency, it is good to find out which medical facilities have 24-hour emergency cardiac care. Also, keep a list of emergency phone numbers next to our phone and with you at all times. Take these steps…NOW!

Warning Signs of a Stroke

Learn the many warning signs of a stroke.

Act FAST and CALL Medical Help IMMEDIATELY

at any sign of a stroke.

Use **F.A.S.T.** to remember warning signs:

F - **FACE:** Ask the person to smile.

Does one side of the face droop?

A - **ARMS:** Ask the person to raise both arms.

Does one arm drift downward?

S - **SPEECH:** Ask the person to repeat a simple phrase.

Is their speech slurred or strange?

T - **TIME:** If you observe any of these signs, note the time.

If given within three hours of the first symptom, there is a clot-buster medication that may reduce long-term disability for the common type of stroke.

A Final Warning:
Remain Positive About Death and Dying

A Loved one's Final Days

Those for whom Providence provides an awareness of their final days are given the blessing and the power to make adjustments and write a new ending to their life's story. Normally, patients and family are shocked at a terminal diagnosis. However, those who take a positive approach to "death and dying" have a totally different outlook and outcome. Death can become the ultimate healing for the patient, their family and friends. A certain level of peace and forgiveness should be part of a loved one's final days. From God's perspective, the moment of death for a believer is a valued and treasured experience. *"Precious in the sight of the Lord is the death of His saints."* (Psalm 116:15).

Memorable Moments

As a loved one gradually loses strength and surrenders to a terminal illness, there can be memorable moments of affection, forgiveness, and sharing of life and living. As a loved one and family gradually face the inevitable, there is a softening of voices, a lessening of inner turmoil, and a willingness to face the future with confidence. Discussions of past times and places and experiences with certain people can produce a positive disposition to act responsibly and bring a positive attitude about the current situation and the future.

A Period of Reconciliation

A terminal illness provides space, time, and opportunity to complete certain unfinished aspects of reconciliation. It has been said, "Our time on earth is to prepare for life after death." Since this truism is deep-seated in the human psychic, it often makes the final period of life of great value to all concerned. A terminal diagnosis provides time for healing old wounds, reconciling relationships, and preparing the soul for the afterlife. Short chats about failures, disappointments, moments of anger, or misdeeds can create an atmosphere of forgiveness that can heal a wounded spirit. No family or individual is without fault and a terminal diagnosis may provide opportunity for apologies, requests for forgiveness, and expressions of frank and honest affection. Such a period of reconciliation can produce agreement to an amicable truce and open the door for an improved understanding of the past and appreciation for a longstanding relationship. The difficulty here is that "reconciliation requires positive movement by all concerned."

The Connectedness of Family

Blood kin and family connections are not always smooth. A sense of closeness often breeds contempt, jealousy, competition, and at times misunderstanding, resentment, and even bitterness. A terminal illness provides time for everyone to "grow up" and be mature adults. The better angels of human nature should rise up and signal that "we" are all here to make this transition smooth and seamless. Each individual in the family has value in the family structure and becomes an essential part in the final celebration of life and the human finality of dying. The family must demonstrate they are moral and ethical citizens of earth before they can be seen as mystical citizens of heaven. It is important for a person suffering a terminal illness to see the connectedness of family as good, nourishing, and supportive.

Memories are Growing Gifts

Meaningful memories are growing gifts that continue to nourish a family. Remembering, the good times, accepting the bad times, and understanding the difference is part of mature family life. Gratitude is commonly expressed by the terminally ill. There is expressed appreciation for companionship and even thankfulness for the final days which provided opportunities for final thoughts and words of preparation for the afterlife. Since no human being is perfect, most want to make final death bed prayers that bring assurance of Divine Presence and the promise of better life. The whole family should be involved both personally and collectively in prayers around the death bed of a loved one. These are healing moments and excellent memories that sustain a family.

Bibliography

Annotated Bibliography on Ageing

Always use good judgment in evaluating printed material from any source.

Blacher, K. (2013). Asian Americans and Pacific Islanders in the United States Aged 65 Years and Older: Economic Indicators. National Asian Pacific Center on Aging. Disaggregated data suggest that many Asian Americans and Pacific Islander sub-groups are among the most impoverished in the United States.

Carter, Jimmy. (1998). *The Virtues of Aging*. New York: Ballentine. ISBN 0-345-42592-8. A former President of the United States shares personal stories along with his ideas on the challenges and blessings of growing old.

Cerin, E., Mellecker, R., Macfarlane, D.J., et al. (2013). Socioeconomic Status, Neighborhood Characteristics, and Walking Within the Neighborhood Among Older Hong Kong Chinese. Journal of Aging and Health. Researchers find that educational attainment was a more significant determinant of walking than socioeconomic status among Hong Kong elders.

Chopra, Deepak and Simon, David. (2001). *Grow Younger, Live Longer: Ten Steps to Reverse Aging*. Harmony Books. ISBN 0609600796. A step-by-step plan which allows readers to regain an energetic and youthful outlook. In easy- to-follow language, the authors suggest ways to nourish your mind and body, allowing you to forestall, or even reverse, the aging process.

Claflin, Edward (editor). (1998). *Age Protectors: Your Guide to Perpetual Youth*. Emmaus, Pennsylvania: Rodale Press, Inc. ISBN 0-87596-454-0. From the editors of Prevention Health Books, this collection of essays by leading doctors and experts presents methods for increasing longevity and slowing down the aging process. It addresses a number of health problems with practical, step-by-step solutions.

Cowdry EV. (1942) Problems of ageing: biological and medical aspects, 2nd ed, Williams & Wilkins, Baltimore.

Dass, Ram. (2000). Still Here: Embracing Aging, Changing, and Dying. New York: Riverhead Books. ISBN 1-57322-049-3. Sixties icon Ram Dass explores what it means to get older. He looks into the aging process in order to lead readers to a sense of purpose and spirituality. In so doing, he tries to provide a new positive perspective on aging and dying.

Digeronimo, Theresa Foy. (2001). *How to Talk to Your Senior Parents About Really Important Things: Specific Questions and Answers and Useful Things to Say.* San Francisco: Jossey-Bass. ISBN 0787956163. A sensitively written book on how to deal with many difficult issues that boomers are faced with regarding their aging parents. This book is a wonderful tool for improving communication between the generations, providing detailed instructions for bringing up and discussing many topics including money, careers, and health.

Dychtwald, Ken. (1999). *Age Power: How the 21st Century Will Be Ruled by the New Old.* New York: Jeremy P. Tarcher/Putnam. ISBN 0874779545. A leading experts on gerontology explains how the aging of the baby-boomer generation will change the way we all live in the coming years. Dychtwald looks at the role of older people in past societies and shows how and why the "new old" will be different. He identifies some ways in which we might better prepare for this coming wave of Age Power.

Gambone, James. (2000). *Refirement: A Boomer's Guide to Life After 50.* Minneapolis: Kirk House Publishing. ISBN 1886513260. As the title suggests, Gambone advocates putting "fire" into the retirement years. In this book, he calls for an active lifestyle that reflects a person's wants and values. He advises people to live their later years in a way that will give something back to the next generation.

Gaskin, D.J., Thorpe Jr, R.J., McGinty, E.E, et al. (2013). Disparities in Diabetes: The Nexus of Race, Poverty, and Place . American Journal of Public Health Findings from the study suggest that policymakers should address problems created by concentrated poverty to address race disparities in diabetes.

Gibson, H.B. (2000). *Loneliness in Later Life.* New York: St. Martin's Press. ISBN 033392018X. Using the results of a British survey and a collection of autobiographies, Gibson draws some interesting conclusions about loneliness and old age. He finds that being alone is not necessarily a negative thing for many older people and that many people deliberately seek solitude. He looks at loneliness as it has appeared in works of literature through the ages and finds that in today's modern society, older people are much healthier and more active with many more options for living than they had in previous generations.

Henderson, Sallirae. (2000). *A Life Complete: Emotional and Spiritual Growth for Midlife and Beyond.* New York: Scribner. ISBN 0-684-83775-7. Henderson shows how the decisions one makes in middle age can have tremendous bearing on later life. She found that many older people were plagued by regrets and unresolved issues from their youth and middle years. In this book, she presents a plan for getting rid of those unpleasant and unproductive emotions so that old age can be filled with a sense of purpose and serenity.

Liu, J. & Wang, L.N. (2013). Caregivers of Patients With Dementia in Chinese Mainland A Retrospective Analysis. American Journal of

Alzheimer's Disease and Other Dementias. The study finds that the number of publications on Chinese dementia caregivers has rapidly increased since 2006.

Liu, J., Guo, M. & Bern-Klug, M. (2013). Economic Stress Among Adult-Child Caregivers of the Oldest Old in China: The Importance of Contextual Factors. Journal of Cross-Cultural Gerontology. Among other results, researchers find that eldest sons had a higher risk of reporting economic stress than other sons and daughters.

Ma, Y., Hébert, J.R., Balasubramanian, R., et al. (2013). All-Cause, Cardiovascular, and Cancer Mortality Rates in Postmenopausal White, Black, Hispanic, and Asian Women With and Without Diabetes in the United States: The Women's Health Initiative, 1993-2009. American Journal of Epidemiology. The study is one of the first to examine racial/ethnic disparities in mortality outcomes among postmenopausal women with and without diabetes

Miller, James E. (1997). *Welcoming Change: Discovering Hope in Life's Transitions.* Minneapolis: Augsburg. ISBN 0-8066-3338-7. An insightful exploration of change along with simple, affirming suggestions for managing life's transitions. Text interspersed with inspiring quotations.and balanced with full-color nature photographs that suggest hope and strength.

Moody, Harry R. (1998). *The Five Stages of the Soul: Charting the Spiritual Passages That Shape Our Lives.* New York: Doubleday. ISBN 0385486774. Moody finds common ground between the many types of spiritual quests that people embark on in their later lives. He has come up with a 5-step process that he believes encompasses the majority of these efforts. Using stories from everyday life as well as myth and legend, Moody shows us how these journeys can lead us to a fulfilling later life.

Myers, David. (2000). *A Quiet World: Living with Hearing Loss.* New Haven: Yale University Press. ISBN 0300084390. Myers, who himself suffers from gradual hearing loss, looks into the world of the hard-of-hearing. He shows how not being able to hear tends to isolate people from the rest of the world, but reports on numerous medical advances, from surgery to hearing aids which can help those suffering from hearing loss. He gives advice to family and friends of those with hearing loss. on *how to communicate with them.*

Paster, Zorba with Meltsner, Susan. (2001). *The Longevity Code: Your Personal Prescription for a Longer, Sweeter Life.* Clarkson Potter/Publishers. ISBN 0609603604. The popular radio host and physician introduces five spheres of wellness – physical, mental, kinship/social, spiritual, and material – that encompass all aspects of life. Within each sphere, Dr. Paster identifies both "busters," negative lifestyle aspects, and "boosters," positive lifestyle aspects. The book helps identify which "busters" are most detrimental to you and how you can replace them with "boosters" using a clip-out card system.

Pickett, Y.R., Bazelais, K.N., Greenberg, R.L. & Bruce, M.L. (2013). <u>Racial and Ethnic Variation in Home Healthcare Nurse Depression Assessment of Older Minority Patients</u>. International Journal of Geriatric Psychiatry. Findings from the study suggest that interventions designed to improve recognition of depression by community providers may reduce racial differences in positive depression screening rates among older home healthcare patients.

Pipher, Mary Bray. (2000). *Another Country: Navigating the Emotional Terrain of Our Elders.* New York: Riverhead Books. ISBN 1573227846. Psychologist Pipher explains some of the basic psychological differences between today's older persons and their boomer children. She shows that while the kids grew up in an atmosphere of emotional openness, the older generation considered emotional displays a sign of weakness. This book tries to reconcile the two ways of thinking.

Roizen, Michael & Stephenson, Elizabeth Ann. (2001). *RealAge: Are You as Young as You Can Be?* New York: Cliff Street Books. ISBN 0060930756. Roizen, a gerontologist at the University of Chicago, has come up with a method for determining what he calls your "real age," which is either the same or more or less than your actual age according to many factors that are taken into consideration. Once you determine your "real age" using a quiz, you can then read about many things you can do to reduce it. The book focuses on preventative health maintenance and presents its lessons in an easy to follow format.

Rowe, John & Kahn, Robert. (1998). *Successful Aging.* New York: Pantheon Books. ISBN 0-375-40045-1. A compelling presentation of the factors that determine how well we age—the result of the MacAuthur Foundation Study of Aging in America, which shows how to maintain optimum physical and mental strength throughout later life.

Shalomi-Schachter, Zalman & Miller, Ronald S. (1997). *From Age-Ing to Sage-Ing: A Profound New Vision of Growing Older.* New York: Warner Books. ISBN 0446671770. Drawing on a number of religious traditions, Rabbi Shalomi-Schachter guides readers through a re-thinking of what old age should be. He envisions a life of mentoring and sharing knowledge with others. Among other subjects, Shalomi-Schacter emphasizes constructive ways of facing death.

Sorkin, D.H. & Ngo-Metzger, Q. (2013). <u>The Unique Health Status and Health Care Experiences of Older Asian Americans: Research Findings and Treatment Recommendations</u>. Clinical Gerontologist. Researchers find that there is a need for more investigation in a number of areas including patient preferences and the use of community health workers.

Taffet GE, Lakatta EG. (2003) Aging of the Cardiovascular System. In: Principles of Geriatric Medicine and Gerontology, 5th ed, Hazzard WR, Blass JP, Halter JB, et al. (Eds), McGraw-Hill, New York.

Vaillant, George E. (2002). *Aging Well: Surprising Guideposts to a Happier Life from the Landmark Harvard Study of Adult Development.* New York: Little Brown & Company. ISBN 0316989363. Using an unprecedented study which followed 824 subjects from their teens to old age, Vaillant is able to tell us quite a bit about what leads to a happy, healthy life. He is able to show the importance of lifestyle choices, as opposed to a person's background and also offers step-by-step advice for ways to improve.

Vinson, L., Crowther, M., Austin, A. & Guin, S. (2013). African Americans, Mental Health, and Aging. Clinical Gerontologist. Researchers find that there are many areas of mental health research on older African Americans where there is a need for further investigation.

Wei, Jeanne Y. & Levkoff, Sue. (2000) *Aging Well: The Complete Guide to Physical and Emotional Health.* New York: John Wiley and Sons. ISBN 047132678X. *Written by two Harvard Medical School faculty, this book deals with many aspects of how the body ages. It describes in detail a number of body systems, telling about the changes that the aging process brings. The book also includes strategies for dealing with age-related problems.*

Willcox, Bradley J.; Willcox, D. Craig; & Suzuki, Makoto. (2001). The Okinawa Program: How the World's Longest-Lived People Achieve Everlasting Health—And How You Can Too. New York: Clarkson Potter Publishers. ISBN 0-609-60747-2. Based on a landmark 25 year study of centenarians, this book shows how the Okinawans have become the longest-lived population in the world. It lays out an easy-to-follow plan, which includes diet, exercise and lifestyle changes which will help readers increase their chances of living longer, too.

Wolfelt, Alan. (1997). The Journey Through Grief: Reflections on Healing. Fort Collins, CO: Companion Press. ISBN 1-879651-11-4. Information-packed yet brief reflection that provides a healing balm and source of empowerment for mourners as well as much-needed insight for professional caregivers.

Supplemental Reading and Resources on Ageing

Adelson, R. (2013). _Staying power: Age-proof your home for comfort, safety and style_. Thornhill, Ont: Sage Tree Pub.

Alexander, Brigitte. "Living Near the End of Life: Queries for the Elderly." _Friends Journal,_ 2009 October http://www. friendsjournal.org/living-near-end-life-queries-elderly

Andrews, Elsie M. "Facing and Fulfilling the Later Years." _Pendle Hill Pamphlet_ 157, 1968. Concerned with the wise and happy use of the later years.

Backstrom, Kirsten. "In Beauty: A Quaker Approach to End of Life Care." _Pendle Hill Pamphlet_ 355, 2001. Hospice nurse and Friend shares stories of experiences in her meeting to show how our dying can be as fully centered on God as our living.

Bacon, Margaret Hope. _Year of Grace: A Novel._ Philadelphia: Quaker Press of Friends General Conference, 2002. The story of a 76 year old Quaker grandmother who learns that she has a year left to live, and her spirit and action-filled last adventure.

Ball, S. (2012). _Livable communities for aging populations: Urban design for longevity_. Hoboken, NJ: John Wiley & Sons.

Berman, C. (2006). _Caring for yourself while caring for your aging parents: How to help, how to survive_, 3rd ed. New York: Henry Holt. (Call Number: 20.9 .B4 2006)

Bien, Peter. "On Retiring to Kendal (and Beyond): A Literary Excursion." _Pendle Hill Pamphlet_ 368, 2003. Retired professor uses literary passages to reflect on whether death is "an unmitigated calamity."

Britain Yearly Meeting, Committee on Eldership and Oversight, _Funerals and Memorial Meetings._ London: Quaker Books, 2003. "This handbook clearly sets out tasks of funeral coordinators and people responsible for eldership and oversight, gives information on low-cost and `green' funerals, has tips on planning for a funeral and has a section for planning for one's own funeral. Includes a form at the back for one to fill out in preparation for your own death. Though some information is pointedly for British Quakers, American Friends will find much that speaks to their condition here as well."

Britain Yearly Meeting, Spirituality and Ageing Group. *This is who I am: Listening with Older Friends.* London: Quaker Books, 2001. "The Spirituality & Aging Group was formed by some older Quakers who were reaching a new phase of life, and were struggling to understand the lessons of old age, and its challenges. This book will be useful for those responsible for pastoral care in Quaker meetings and elsewhere and to people of all ages who listen to each other in love and friendship."

Center for Mental Health Services. (2005). *Mentally healthy aging: A report on overcoming stigma for older Americans*. Rockville, MD: U.S. Dept. of Health and Human Services, Substance Abuse and Mental Health Services Administration, Center for Mental Health Services. (Call Number: 23 .C4 .M46)

De Grey, Aubrey D.N.J (2007). "Life Span Extension Research and Public Debate: Societal Considerations". *Studies in Ethics, Law, and Technology.*

Friends Journal: Quaker Thought and Life Today. Special issue on Aging and Life's End, July 2004. Articles available online: http://www.friendsjournal.org/issue/july-2004

Gaffney, Amy Runge. "God's Healing Spirit: An Answer to Suffering." *Quaker Life*, December 2000. Reflections on her physician father's death. http://www.fum.org/QL/issues/0012/suffering.htm

Gates, Tom. "You Must Live a Dying Life": Reflections on Human Mortality and the Spiritual Life. Boston: Beacon Hill Friends House, 2007. "I want to explore with you the subject of death: how our mortality is the central issue in our spiritual lives, at one and the same time a stumbling block and an invitation to transformation; how our mortality isolates us, from one another and from God, but at the same time unites us, with all humanity and with the divine mystery that is both our source and our destiny; and how it is that caring for the dying among us can open us as perhaps nothing else to this mystery and transformation."

Gaventa, W. C., & Coulter, D. L.. (2005). *End-of-life care: Bridging disability and aging with person-centered care*. Binghamton, NY: Haworth Pastoral Press. (Call Number: 33 .G3)

Green, Connie McPeak. "To Live Fully Until Death: Lessons from the Dying." In *Friends Journal: Quaker Thought and Life Today*. Special issue on Aging and Life's End, July 2004. Featured essay available from *Friends Journal* website: http://www.friendsjournal.org/live-fully-until-death-lessons-dying

Hayflick, Leonard. *How and Why We Age* (1996) A good book on aging. It is seven-handed and discusses the discoveries recently made about the aging process. Hayflick provides evidence behind various theories of aging.

Jacob, Norma. "Growing Old: A View from Within." *Pendle Hill Pamphlet* 239, 1981. Reflections on aging based on her experiences, thoughts and observance of others, from a retired social worker living at Kendal-at-Longwood. Download from Pendle Hill: http://www.pendlehill.org/resources/files/pdf%20files/php239b.pdf

Lampen, Diana. *Facing Death.* Imprint Systems Ltd., Wanganui, NZ, 1996. On death, bereavement and the need for truth telling.

Lewis, Claude E. "How Do I Love Thee?: A Marriage Survives Alzheimer's." *Quaker Life*, June 1999. Reflections from a Quaker dentist on his wife's diagnosis of Alzheimer's. http://www.fum.org/QL/issues/9906/lewis.htm

Lyman, Mary Redington. "Death and the Christian Answer." *Pendle Hill Pamphlet* 107, 1960 In the face of our society's general denial about death, hers is an appreciation of mortality, an explanation of Christ's holistic life giving assurances based on faith and God's love.

MacKinlay, E. (2008). *Ageing, disability, and spirituality: Addressing the challenge of disability in later life*. Philadelphia: Jessica Kingsley Publishers. (Call Number: 46 .M3)

Marshall, Jay W. "I am not Healed Yet!" *Quaker Life,* November 1998. Reflections on grief and healing after the loss of a loved one.http://www.fum.org/QL/issues/9811/marshall.htm

McGuire, F. A., Boyd, R. K., & Tedrick, R. E. (2004). *Leisure and aging: Ulyssean living in later life* (3rd ed.). Champaign, IL: Sagamore Pub. (Call Number: 40.9 .M34 2004)

McIver, Lucy. "Song of Death, Our Spiritual Rebirth: A Quaker Way of Dying." *Pendle Hill Pamphlet* 340, 1998. On the witness to the power of God to be present in each moment of life, and especially the moment of death.

Morrison, Mary C. "Gift of Days: Report of an Illness." *Pendle Hill Pamphlet* 364, 2003, At age 92, the author relates the gift of her extraordinary experience of 100 days of illness, near-death and slow recovery.

Morrison, Mary C. "Without Nightfall Upon the Spirit." *Pendle Hill Pamphlet* 311, 1994. "To preside over the disintegration of one's own body, looking on as sight and hearing, strength, speed, and short-term memory deteriorate, calls for a heroism that is no less impressive for being quiet and patient..." Octogenarian's writings on the demands and joys of aging and on recognizing the source of dignity and ways to nurture the integrity of aging.

Morrison, Mary C. *Let Evening Come: Reflections on Aging.* NY: Doubleday, 1998. Expanded version of "Without Nightfall Upon the Spirit."

Mullen, Tom. "Two Funerals and a Party." *Quaker Life*, September/October 2009. Reflections on memorial services. http://www.fum.org/QL/issues/0909/TwoFuneralsandaParty.htm

Mullen, Tom. "When Friends Say Goodbye." *Quaker Life*, April 2000. Reflections on death and memorial services and on the memorial service for Mullen's wife . http://www.fum.org/QL/issues/0004/mullen.htm

Mullen, Tom. *Living Longer and Other Sobering Possibilities.* Richmond, IN: Friends United Press, 1996. Humorous treatment of growing older, medical problems, and adjusting to new routines for living.

Murphy, Carol. "Milestone 70." *Pendle Hill Pamphlet 287*, 1989. Mystic shares glimpses of her daily life at age 70, inviting us to sense the divine in the ordinary.

Murphy, Carol. "Valley of the Shadow." *Pendle Hill Pamphlet 184*, 1972. Reflections on the ultimate problem of death what the living make of it.

Nuland, Sherwin B. (2007). *The Art of Aging: A Doctor's Prescription for Well-Being,*Random House

Nuland, Sherwin B. (1994) *How We Die:: Reflections of Life's Final Chapter, New Edition,* Vintage Books, NY.

Papalia, Diane. Olds, Sally W., Feldman, Ruth D. (2004) "Physical and Cognitive Development in Late Adulthood". *Human Develo*p**ment. Mc-Graw Hill.**

Phillips, Judith, Kristine Ajrouch, and Sarah Hillcoat-Nallétamby (2010), *Key Concepts in Social Gerontology* (SAGE Publications,) 12-13.

Pies R. The anatomy of sorrow: a spiritual, phenomenological, and neurological perspective. Philos Ethics Humanit Med. 2008; 3: 17. Accessed at: http://www.ncbi.nlm.nih.gov/pmc/articles/PMC2442112/

Quaker Aging Resources.
New York and Philadelphia Yearly Meetings of Friends (Quakers), through generous funding from Friends Foundation for the Aging and the Thomas Scattergood Foundation, collaborated to develop Quaker Aging Resources. The project was designed to assist Meetings and individuals in responding to the needs of aging Friends including age related changes, chronic illness or disability. The resources are intended to uphold a culture of care for the body, mind, spirit and community of the individual which is consistent with our Quaker faith. http://www.quakeragingresources.org/

Richards, M. (2009). *Caresharing: A reciprocal approach to caregiving and care receiving in the complexities of aging, illness or disability.* Woodstock, VT: SkyLight Paths Pub. (Call Number: 54 .R5)

Scott-Maxwell, Florida. *The Measure of My Days.* London: Stuart & Watkins, 1968. Playwright and Jungian analyst Florida Scott-Maxwell explores the unique predicament of one's later years: when one feels both cut off from the past and out of step with the present; when the body rebels at activity but the mind becomes more passionate than ever.

Smith, Bradford. "Dear Gift of Life: A Man's Encounter with Death." *Pendle Hill Pamphlet* 142, 1965. Journal and poetry of a Friend facing death from cancer.

Southeastern Yearly Meeting, *Dying, Death and Bereavement*, approved, 2001
Six-page draft of SEYM Faith and Practice chapter on dying, death and bereavement available online at: http://www.seym.org/FP.pdf/DyingDeathBereavement.pdf

Stafford, P. B. (2009). *Elderburbia: Aging with a sense of place in America*. Santa Barbara, CA: Praeger. (Call Number: 20.9 .S7)

Stuart-Hamilton, Ian (2006). *The Psychology of Ageing: An Introduction*. London: Jessica Kingsley Publishers.

Waddington, Mary. "Gifts From the Closet." In *Friends Journal: Quaker Thought and Life Today*. Special issue on Aging and Life's End, 2004 July. Available from *Friends Journal* website: http://www.friendsjournal.org/gifts-closet

Walsh, P. N., & LeRoy, B. (2004). *Women with disabilities aging well: A global view*. Baltimore:

Yungblut, John. "For that Solitary Individual: An Octogenarian's Counsel on Living and Dying." *Pendle Hill Pamphlet* 316, 1994. On becoming a contemplative later in life.

Yungblut, John. "On Hallowing One's Diminishments." *Pendle Hill Pamphlet* 292, 1990. Describes the experience of contemplative prayer in facing diminishments from birth defects, natural disasters, aging, and death.

Zisook S, Simon N, Reynolds C, Pies R, Lebowitz, B, Tal-Young, I, Madowitz, J, Shear, MK. Bereavement, Complicated Grief, and DSM, Part 2: Complicated Grief. J Clin Psychiatry. 2010;71(8): 1097-8.

— **Most books are available through Amazon.com.**

ABOUT THE AUTHOR

*S*ubesh Ramjattan, DHL, DLitt, is a Renaissance man searching for knowledge and reaching for truth from any source. Among honors, he holds two honoris casa degrees from distinguished universities for his philanthropy, human service endeavors, and the contribution his five (6) substantive books made to the formal literature of the Caribbean. His life journey began in a poor village learning common-sense lessons from family and the village environment. He proceeded to learn more through education and as a young man working to gain the knowledge and resources to become a prosperous businessman. Throughout his life, he has sought to connect the dots of the present with the lessons of the past to understand present moral and social issues. He listens attentively and reads constantly. Subesh remembers almost everything good he learns from any source. He is unselfish in support of worthy projects and demonstrates concern for the underprivileged by providing programs and projects which enable the disadvantaged to become moral citizens of the Nation.

Subesh is a serious student of all subjects that touch his life. When he discovers the interrelationship of concepts and constructs, he immediately connects the dots by looking backwards to lessons already learned to inform his discourse with others. This interest has resulted in a business and personal journey that has increased the quality of life for many. His first book, The *Anapausis Partnership*, co-authored with his wife, Debra, catalogued much of the business and spiritual journey that established a model of philanthropy, mentoring, and coaching to improve the quality of life for the disadvantaged of Trinidad and Tobago.

Dr. Ramjattan's second book, *God's Work Done God's Way*, revealed more of his passion for ethical and morally based assistance for the disadvantaged. His third book, *Living a Life Larger than Yourself*, dealt with the quality of life he desired for all of God's children from the cradle to the grave. His fourth book, *Navigating the Challenges of Faith-based Behavior*, was a sincere effort to reach family, friends and colleagues with the values that reflect Divine influence and moral values on a personal lifestyle. His sixth book, *Adversity Leads to Achievement*, shined light on a common-sense lesson: difficulties can be stepping stones to a positive future.

This Second Edition of his fifth book, *Ageing has a Silver Lining – Coping with Rainy Days*, is a crowning achievement to his work with the disadvantaged and covers many aspects of ageing and the supportive processes for the elderly. Specifically, it deals with the difficulties of the ageing process, senior living problems, and the need for adequate eldercare and senior living facilities. This included the planning and construction of Olive's House – a four stage project for the care of the elderly dedicated January 2014. Perhaps the most meaningful aspect of the life of Subesh Ramjattan is that all credit is given to divine blessings and he freely shares these blessings with others. Subesh continues to influence, speak, and mentor to improve the quality of life of others.

More data is available:

subesh60@gmail.com or (868) 354 -7319

Dr. Ramjattan's years of service were recognized by several international organizations, most recently being:

♦ The International Third World Leaders Association awarded him the KINGDOM STATESMAN AWARD for 2011. This award was given for leadership which demonstrated maturity, quality and character as a Statesman and more than 30-years of distinguished service.

♦ HUMANeX VENTURES honored him as a COMMUNITY EXEMPLAR in 2013. A Community Exemplar is highlighted by a life of significant impact, multiplied through thousands of those that they impact directly and indirectly, in ways that will live beyond the present and be felt, modeled, and multiplied for many, many years - a rich legacy for generations. According to HUMANeX VENTURES those who receive this award are:

- Activators of change
- Catalysts in making a difference
- Craftsmen of their trade
- Creators of meaning in their lives and in others
- Developers of talent and potential
- Doers and Dreamers
- Dream makers
- Educators
- High achievers
- Impact and Legacy Builders.
- Influencers
- Innovators
- Listeners
- Masters with a purpose
- Motivators
- Multipliers
- Passionate to teach and lead
- Role models of Excellence

♦ Global Educational Advance, Inc. admitted Dr. Ramjattan with all rights and privileges to the ORDER OF MEPHIBOSHETH on July 27, 2013, recognizing his understanding that each child is different and honoring his faithful following of faith-based principles and unselfish investing of resources and energy to build bridges of hope and care for disadvantaged children.

♦ In January 2014 at the dedication of Olive's House, Dr. Ramjattan was honored for his leadership and contribution.

♦ In the summer of 2014, growing out of concern for the needs of women, an initiative Global Women's Inter-reliant NETWORK, was launched to cultivate the Divine Nurturing Attribute of Women in Trinidad and Tobago and the Caribbean region.

♦ On 31 August 2014, His Excellency Anthony Thomas Aquinas Carmona, O.R.T.T., S.C., President and Commander-in-Chief of the Armed forces of the Republic of Trinidad and Tobago, did award Subesh Ramjattan The Humming Bird Medal (Bronze) for Community Service.

♦ In the fall of 2014, the Anapausis Community initiated the ANAPAUSIS Together Strong NETWORK, a strategy to organize men for moral excellence and transparency in belief and conduct and cultivate mutual support for others.

♦ In October 2014, The University of the West Indies recognized the contribution Dr. Ramjattan had made to the literature and the people of Trinidad and Tobago with the awarding of the Doctor of Letters (DLitt).

♦ Draft copy of Dr. Ramjattan's Speech at the Graduation ceremony at the St. Augustine campus of UWI to the Faculty of Medical Science October 2014. (See copy below)

Take Back the Moral High Ground

Greetings to all! (with normal protocols observed)

Many professionals have become accustomed to the "moral darkness" and often do not see the specific needs of the community around them. When it comes to morality and ethics, charity and generosity in support of the needy, we must **take back the moral high ground** clearly held by those who established this Nation. Since you are launching a career in the field of medicine, I challenge you to both review and honor the oldest binding document in your historic field of study, the Hippocratic Oath. It is a system of moral principles that apply values and judgments to the practice of medicine, a most honorable profession.

Those with expertise and resources must join the effort to make moral citizens of the children and solicit the assistance of the business community and non-profit entities to join the government to meet the needs of all citizens. We must get professionals, parents, faith-based entities, community leaders, and elected officials reading the same page and singing the same tune to demonstrate a spirit of cooperation.

We must utilize the expertise and energy of all professions in assisting the present and the next generation. It is immoral to avoid this responsibility; it is less than humane to fail in our responsibility to the generation that brought us into this world, invested in our growing years, gave us a moral compass, provided the encouragement for an adequate education, and gave us a boost to grow into productive citizens. To withhold care or resources from children, the poor, and needy seniors is a gross injustice and a moral blight on any society. We must **take back the moral high ground!**

My personal concern for the less fortunate came from frequent statements by my mother: she would often say things like, **"Never look down at someone unless you are willing to help them get up."** This instilled in me a passionate commitment to assist the less fortunate, especially neglected children, dysfunctional families, those with limited access to higher education, and the elderly in need of housing and care. I see this as a moral obligation. All professionals should remember that **opportunity equals obligation**.

Perhaps the historic professions of religion, law and medicine have the most opportunities to meet this moral obligation. One must never pass up an opportunity to assist others on their journey. We must all develop a sense of duty and responsibility to **take back the moral high ground** so nobly established by the early leaders of this Nation. We owe a debt for our own upbringing. Not just a sense of indebtedness, but a grateful heart for family, the opportunity for education, good friends and a stable government. We must all become aware of the opportunities around us to make a difference. And remember, **"You don't have to make news headlines to make a difference in the lives of others."**

"Keep on Keeping On" is a song on the album, **_Roots_** written by Curtis Mayfield. He was a song writer in the early Civil Rights Movement who focused his lyrics on social problems and personal responsibility. A typical verse in his lyrics was:

> _We who are young, should now take a stand_
> _Don't run from the burdens of women and men._
> _Continue to give, continue to live_
> _For what you know is right._

- Curtis Mayfield was telling his generation to take a **stand for what was right**
- He was warning them **not to run from the burdens or responsibility** of the clear task at hand.
- This task included the "burdens" of both women and men.

- His challenge was to **continue to give and continue to live** for what they knew was right.

- In other words, his music **was an ethical and moral challenge** to the current generation to keep moving forward with the push for equality and **to make a difference by doing what was lawful and right.**

If we understand the legacy of our Founders and what they expressed in the Flag, the pledge to the flag, and the words of the National Song, we would be reminded of both our roots and our wings.

One of the patriotic songs of Trinidad and Tobago is **"God Bless Our Nation"** by Marjorie Padmore that was adopted as the **National Song**. Let's look at the last verse of the lyrics:

God bless our leaders give them grace to guide
Bestow on them thy judgment wise to rule our land aright
To keep the flag of freedom high that we may sing most lustily
We take a pride in Our Liberty.

An honest review of the words of the **Pledge** to our Flag should be a constant challenge to all; it has many elements similar to the Hippocratic Oath.

PLEDGE TO OUR FLAG

I solemnly pledge to dedicate my life
To the service of my God and my country.
I will honour my parents, my teachers,
My leaders and my elders,
And those in authority.

I will be clean and honest
In all my thoughts, my words and my deeds
I will strive in everything I do,
To work together with my fellow man
Of every creed and race,
For the greater happiness of all
And the honour and glory of my country.

Each journey begins with a first step. In reality it is the little things that count in life. When the first man landed on the moon, he said, **"One small step for (a) man; one giant step for mankind."** It took decades of planning and labour, with many people working long hours to put that machine and that man on the moon. They paid the price, did the work, and made a significant contribution to mankind. That is where we stand in the Republic of Trinidad and Tobago today. Will you join the men and women of good will and take the necessary steps and encourage the government to do their part and through a cooperative effort **take back the moral high ground** and move our people and our Nation forward into the "light" of reality. Dare we do less?

There is a story about an old man in a small town, called the "Lamplighter." Early each night he would go to each street corner and light the gas lamp. The old gas lamps made only a small light on the dark street. As the Lamplighter went from street to street it appeared that he was **knocking holes in the darkness**. This is an example of what one person can do. And a good example of what one in the medical profession can do as they daily strive to knock holes in the darkness and enlighten those they serve.

The big questions today are simple:

"What **have you** done?" — "What **can you do** differently?"

"What **can you do** better?" — "What **can you do** new?"

Or perhaps a better question would be: **"What will you do to make a difference in the lives of those you serve and ensure the health and prosperity of this Nation?**

I leave you with one of my favorite quotes from the wisdom of Mahathma Gandhi:

> *"Don't dwell on those who let you down;*
> *cherish those who lift you up!"*

Keep on doing what you know is right and those things which will make a significant difference for your family, your profession, and the Nation. **May Providence guide you personally and empower your professional journey.**

Books By the Author

May be ordered through:

www.gea-books.com *(Author's Page)*
subesh60@gmail.com

Amazon, Barnes&Noble, Espresso Book Machines, or anywhere good books are sold.

The Anapausis Partnership
— **A Model of Philanthropy, Mentoring, and Coaching**
ISBN: 978-1-935434-49-8

The book deals with common-sense lessons and faith-based principles that result in a model of Philanthropy, Mentoring, and Coaching. It is a "How To" treatise in building both a relationship and advancing an agenda that benefits children, couples, faith-based groups, NGO'S, non-profit organizations, and family life. It is a true story of two individuals, who found each other amid their inspired mission to assist their homeland. It is a narrative of love and work, faith and worship, sacrament and service, stewardship and charity, teamwork and faithfulness. The pages are filled with commonsense lessons that are later translated into faith-based principles and used to advance many projects for the benefit of the poor and needy.

God's Work Done God's Way
— **You Don't Have to Make Headlines to Make a Difference**
ISBN: 978-1-935434-60-3

Some see faith as a "vending machine," but the author shows not only the benefits of a faith-based life, but the obligations faith-based people to accomplish their work with guidance from Providence. He believes that to live a life with purpose and significance will be a good life that benefits others. This book presents a lifestyle that cares for the disadvantaged and meets the challenge to get others involved. Quality thoughts and moral values come from believing and behaving learned principles. It is not what one gather, but what is scatter that defines the quality of life.

Living a Life Larger Than Yourself
ISBN: 978-1-935434-62-7

The word "happiness" as it is used today it relies on the little word "hap" which means "good luck or by chance." Happenstance does not create a quality of life. Only purposeful behavior that is more than activities can bring the deep satisfaction of "happiness." Quality of life should not be confused with the standard of living, which is primarily income. The term "quality of life," as revealed in this book, is our positive intervention in the lives of the less fortunate.

Navigating the Challenges of Faith-based Behavior
— Conduct that Exhibits a Moral Course in Life
ISBN: 978-1-935434-64-1

A faith-based lifestyle determines both the course of action, the destination of the journey and provides a standard of behavior. Lifestyle provides intentionality of conduct and enables one to behave in a planned and deliberate way. The wise man Solomon was concerned about an empty life without permanent value that leads to frustration. He wrote, **"Pursue your course but know that God will judge your behavior."** (Ecclesiastes 11.9 DOT) The value of a charted course relates to both the terminal objective and the time one has to travel toward stated goals. The design of this book illustrates in a nautical/sailing ship framework that there is a difference between **believe** and **behave**.

Ageing Has a Silver Lining
— Coping with Rainy Days
ISBN 978-1-935434-65-8

The purpose of the book is to improve the quality of life for seniors as they span the ageing process and move to their final decade of graceful ageing. The author deals with the difficulties of the ageing process, the senior living problems, the need for adequate eldercare facilities, and compassionate end of life care. The objective is to ensure a Silver Lining to the clouds that surround the ageing process for seniors and their caregivers.

Adversity Leads to Achievement
— **Learning to Surmount Difficulties**
ISBN: 978-1-935434-81-8

With a tearful family parting and five dollars in his pocket, the author was asked by his father to make a simple promise: "Never steal from anyone." Contained in the limited family resources represented by the five dollars and the moral promise never to take advantage of others by stealing was the essence of morality for Dr. Ramjattan's life and practice of business. Lessons learned from parents and siblings growing up in a rural village, together with his education, work experience, and interpersonal communications in the wider world, taught him to overcome difficulties: that adversity could ultimately produce achievement. It is such lessons that prepare young men and women to become productive citizens. All the recorded accomplishments of history were the result of such learned lessons used to make achievements in spite of adversities and their accomplishments changed the world for the better. These commonsense lessons became faith-based principles to guide the author's life and profession. They were used to create programs, construct buildings, change the hopes and dreams of disadvantaged children, restore dysfunctional families, provide age-specific education, and practical community service for those willing to learn. Such commonsense lessons are transferrable and reproducible in other venues. By sharing these lessons, Dr. Ramjattan hopes to make a difference in the lives of families, communities, and society.

Content Guide

- Diet
- Nature's color-coded fruits and vegetables
- Weight
- Exercise
- Stress

- Loved Ones Remain Loved
- Away -- but in our Hearts
- Find Strength in Serving
- Giving and Sharing
- Intrinsic vs. Extrinsic Rewards
- Enjoy the Benefits
- Golden Memories
- Bright Side of Clouds